# A
# Certain Blind Man

# A
# Certain Blind Man

AND OTHER ESSAYS ON
THE AMERICAN MOOD

BY

*Robert E. Fitch*

*Essay Index Reprint Series*

BOOKS FOR LIBRARIES PRESS
FREEPORT, NEW YORK

Library of Congress Cataloging in Publication Data

Fitch, Robert Elliot, 1902-
    A certain blind man.

    (Essay index reprint series)
    1.  U. S.--Intellectual life.  2.  U. S.--Foreign
relations--20th century.  I.  Title.
E169.1.F55  1972          917.3'03'9          75-142628
ISBN 0-8369-2549-1

PRINTED IN THE UNITED STATES OF AMERICA
BY
NEW WORLD BOOK MANUFACTURING CO., INC.
HALLANDALE, FLORIDA 33009

*To the*
*Living Spirit*
*of*
*My Father and My Mother*

# PREFACE

THE Second World War descended upon the American people like Augustinian divine grace —prevenient, irresistible, and indispensable. It was prevenient, because we sought it not, and could not foretell its coming. It was irresistible, because, even though we would, we could not cast it off when it did come upon us. And it might be said to have been indispensable in that, at this time, and under these circumstances, it is hard to conceive what other event might have had the force to awaken us from our spiritual lethargy. But whether, in the double election that attends such an occasion, we are to be chosen for salvation or for damnation, I am enough of an Arminian to believe that our free will shall in part decide.

These essays, then, are an inquiry into the spiritual heritage, the present spiritual condition, and the spiritual destiny of the American people. The first three essays deal with our present spiritual condition; the other two, with our spiritual heritage and spiritual destiny. Naturally, this writing is directed to the reader in his more serious moods. When his moods are more frivolous, he may still find solace by turning to light summer romances, or to text-books on the economic system.

vii

Either one of these forms of fiction has its justification as a means of momentary escape from the disturbing complexities of life on this earth. But, when we are confronted again by reality, it is time to return from fiction to truth, from economics to theology.

Some critics may protest that what I call the "culture of complacency" is no longer descriptive of the present spiritual condition of the American people. Let me say, then, that the complacency with which I am concerned is not a complacency in the presence of the fact of war. So far, what the war has revealed of the temper of the American people is matter for congratulation rather than for condemnation. The complacency with which I am concerned is our complacency in time of peace. In retrospect, it is humiliating to consider that complacency during the last two decades of peace, and, in prospect, it is terrifying to contemplate the possibility of the resurgence of that complacency in the peace that shall follow the war.

It would be comforting to believe that, because we have changed the character of our conduct, we have also changed the character of our ideals. But the spiritual condition of a people is not so easily transformed as are its overt actions. External circumstances may compel us to new modes of behavior, while the old ways of thinking and of believing lie deeply embedded in our minds and in our souls. The sow that was washed returns to her wallowing. And, while the *mores* of complacency may be held in abeyance during the brief but valorous season of war, it is too probable that they shall re-assert themselves in the spiritual let-down after the emergency.

These *mores*, though they have been supported too often by the Christian clergy, have no part in our Christian heritage. They are the expression, rather, of a bourgeois culture with its delight in pleasure, profits, comfort, peace, ease, and isolation. Their chief spokesman is, not the priest, but the economist. In a business civilization, the economist is the approved peddler of panaceas and dispenser of opiates for the people. Always bland and unctuous, whether discoursing on the glorious anarchies of a *laissez-faire* capitalism, or extolling the classical symmetry of a communist pattern, he is the official metaphysician of a materialistic age. So well have our minds been softened by the sweet pap of his smooth doctrine that, nowadays, one thinks that the chief recommendation for any idealistic, or humanitarian, program is the evidence that it rests on sound considerations in economics; although, to the truly critical mind, this evidence should be the first warning to view that program with suspicion. For it is the economist who has taught us to believe that, in disregard of the soul of a civilization, one needs only a little tinkering with the mechanism, or the creation of a brand new mechanism, and everything will be all right. Whatever his differences with his colleagues, he recognizes but one ultimate orthodoxy—the orthodoxy of optimism.

The economist, indeed, is always a utopian. He is a utopian because he is a materialist. It is always easier to envisage a change in the material furniture of the world, than to effect a radical alteration of its spiritual condition. The task of the interior decorator, in transforming the physical appearance of a home, is always a simpler one than the task of the religionist in transforming the moral condition of its inhabitants. But it has been a part of our sentimentalism to believe that, when the interior decorator was done with his work on the furnishings, then the other change would follow by automatic reflex. Actually, the task of the interior decorator is a simple one only when it is abstracted from the setting of human prejudices, and passions, and aspirations, in which it must be performed. It is this act of abstraction, done once for all, which enables the economist to display, on his brow, that peace and serenity as of a spirit from another world.

This writing, then, is, in part, a protest against the unregenerate sentimentalism of a materialistic culture, and, in part, a summons to return to the more arduous idealism of our Christian heritage. If there is any philosophy of history implicit in these pages, it stems from Amos rather than from Adam Smith, from Augustine rather than from Karl Marx. The author believes that, if we are to satisfy our present craving for reality, then we must give up the specious deceptions of a purely secular wisdom, and find our larger home in the ample tradition of Christianity, with its great, historic insights into the nature and destiny of man. The reality that we find here will be, in Niebuhr's phrase, a reality that is

"beyond tragedy," in that it will not let us be easily
disillusioned, because it will not allow us to believe that
the good can be purchased at a price cheaper than the
cross; and in that it will not permit us to suffer perma-
nent defeat, because it reveals to us a power which,
though seemingly crushed on the cross, does yet tower
over all the wrecks of time while informing its nobler
and more enduring monuments.

In conclusion—without wishing to implicate any one
in the opinions expressed here—I should like to make
acknowledgment to a few persons to whom I owe much:
To John Dewey, to whose writings, in spite of some
things said in these pages, I owe everything in the way
of philosophic discipline and method. To Reinhold
Niebuhr, chief of the prophets of the Lord in our time.
To John Herman Randall, Jr., who taught me many
things. And to John C. Bennett, for friendly offices and
counsels.

Occidental College,
Los Angeles, California,
April 6th, 1943.

# Contents

*One:*

# A CERTAIN
# BLIND MAN

*And it came to pass, that as he was come nigh unto Jericho,
a certain blind man sat by the way side begging: And hearing
the multitude pass by, he asked what it meant. And they told
him, that Jesus of Nazareth passeth by.*

*And he cried, saying, Jesus, thou son of David, have mercy
on me. And they which went before rebuked him, that he
should hold his peace: but he cried so much the more, Thou
son of David, have mercy on me.*

*And Jesus stood, and commanded him to be brought unto
him: and when he was come near, he asked him, saying, What
wilt thou that I shall do unto thee? And he said, Lord, that I
may receive my sight. And Jesus said unto him, Receive thy
sight: thy faith hath saved thee.*

*Luke 18:35–43.*

*And Jesus said, For judgment I am come into this world,
that they which see not might see; and that they which see
might be made blind.*

*And some of the Pharisees which were with him heard
these words, and said unto him, Are we blind also? Jesus said
unto them, If ye were blind, ye should have no sin: but now ye
say, We see; therefore your sin remaineth.*

*John 9:39–41.*

# 1:

A CERTAIN
BLIND MAN

ONE of the curious diseases that plagued the American people during the months before their entry into the Second World War was a pathetic disbelief in their own powers of judgment—in their ability to distinguish truth from falsehood, to discriminate the good from the bad. A pat title for this ailment would have been the "propaganda psychosis." It was exhibited in uncritical suspicion of all news reports and all editorial opinions concerning current events, in scrupulous avoidance of free discussion of contemporary issues that had any vital importance, and in an introverted concentration upon minding one's own business to the exclusion of the affairs of the world at large. Its peculiar pathology was especially revealed in the attitude toward the British. The fact that the British—having learned a thing or two from the First World War—were both careful and frugal in their use of propaganda in the Second World War, was taken as certain evidence of the ·more Machiavellian and more dangerously insidious character of their methods.

This condition of the American mind might also have been labeled the "three-Japanese-monkeys-psychosis."

Hear no evil! See no evil! Speak no evil!—and, at the same time, Hear no good! See no good! Speak no truth! For those who fear the evil will never learn the good; and those who cannot look upon falsehood and discern its mark will never know the truth.

The situation had its profound irony, in that the general public, while busily straining out the gnats, had already swallowed the camel. This camel was the twenty-year-old propaganda of pacifism and of isolationism. Compared to this well-established propaganda, the more recent machinations of the Nazis, or of "the British, the bankers, and the Bolsheviks," or of "the Jews and international capitalists" were like froth blown before the wind. So thoroughly had its job been done that, probably for the first time in American history, we had an entire generation of young people in college who, from the day of their birth, had drunk in, with their mothers' milk, as it were, the dogmas of peace at any price, and of total abstention from all foreign entanglements. When the crisis came upon us, then, we had the wry spectacle of the most hardened propagandists of the lot—the pacifists and the isolationists— being the most vehement in their denunciation of the menace of propaganda; and of a great part of the public trying to steel its soul against the poison from abroad, while it continued to find congenial to its system the poison it had brewed at home and had been swallowing for some two decades.

The propaganda psychosis, however, was only one

symptom of a deeply rooted cultural disease. This sickness which had come over the spirit, not only of the American people but of all modern peoples, was a profound disbelief in the reality of the mind and of the soul. That these two entities were only the pleasing fictions of an outmoded, pre-scientific theology, had gradually become the unexpressed conviction of millions of modern men and women. Obviously, then, since we are mere robots, we must dread the power of propaganda. For, when we have no mind to tell truth from falsehood, and no soul to discern good from evil, we are inevitably the helpless prey of the most skillful master of manipulative techniques, and are of all creatures the most miserable. Strange it is that not ten years of "progressive education"—not twenty, nor thirty years of it—were enough to cure us of this mortal malady.

And so it came to pass that, as a nation, we were like a certain blind man, which sat by the wayside, begging. Sounding in our ears were all the tumult, and the tears, and the laughter of the passing parade. But whether this buzzing, blooming confusion had in it any meaning—whether, at the cry of distress, we should step forth to help a brother, whether the song of joy were a harbinger of love—whether, indeed, this were at all a humanly significant pageant: that we knew not. Moreover, our beggar was no Oriental Lazarus—unsightly with withered limbs, leprous skin, running sores, broken teeth, and crawling scalp. He was a fat beggar—decked out with the fairest of garments, and bedizened with the jewels of the world's greatest treasure house. Yet, being blind, and so unable to see, he was perforce a beggar—begging for the light!

II

This blindness of the American people was not a congenital blindness. There was a time when we could see. Since then, however, the scales had closed over our eyes. These were the scales of materialism, hedonism, and sentimentalism. They were compounded of a common clay—the dull, rich clay of profits, prosperity, pleasure, comfort, and ease.

It is understandable, then, why the economists have been the official metaphysicians of our time. The matured scholasticism of their thought exhibits all the refinement and comprehensiveness of the *Summa Theologiæ* of Thomas Aquinas; and their pronouncements display that irresponsibility toward the truth and that contempt for elementary fact which are the tokens of the blind arrogance of any priestly caste. The mere detail that there are sects among them from which one may take his choice hardly improves the situation. The classical economists describe for us a world which never has existed, while the radical economists describe for us a world which one hopes to God never shall exist. If one should believe the classical economists, then one must believe that there was a time on this earth when man dwelt as though in very heaven; and, if one should accept the predictions of the radical economists, he must be convinced that there shall be a time on this earth when man shall live as though in very hell. But, be it heaven, or hell—it is yet the Golden Calf which presides over the whole scene—this, the Determiner of Our Destiny!

The final proof of the all-pervasive influence of this theology lies in the need we feel for rationalizing our conduct by economic arguments. To prove that we act out of the profit-motive is to prove that we are both sane and respectable. Even a fascist state like Italy found it necessary to rationalize the conquest of Ethiopia by arguing that it was an economically advantageous venture, although the most rudimentary common sense could see that this was a lie. Adolf Hitler, who was a better fascist than Mussolini, and therefore not subject to the illusions of the bourgeois theology, displayed great shrewdness in utilizing this theology to make respectable, in bourgeois eyes, his schemes for world conquest. To talk about *lebensraum*, and markets, and raw materials, when what one really wanted was the hegemony of the whole earth: even thus could the bourgeois democracies be duped and gulled by their own religion!

Of course, the fact that, in our day, economics has supplied the official sanctions for conduct is no more evidence that the sole interests of life have been economic, than the fact that religion supplied the sanctions in the Middle Ages proves that the interests of life at that time were purely religious. Life is always complex, and human motives are always multifarious. The reigning sanction for conduct simply derives from what is the pre-eminently respectable interest of the time. Moreover, there is a kind of cultural lag, whereby each sanction continues, for a while, to function in a later age, when the pre-eminent interest of mankind is already of another sort. Thus the religious sanction of the Middle Ages continued to operate in the period of the rise of capitalism and of the industrial revolution. And the economic sanction has achieved full self-consciousness just at this moment when its very foundations are being destroyed, and when we are entering upon a new era. The sanctions of the future, we may safely predict, will be political. We shall witness an interesting revival of the political history, so much despised by the rational, bourgeois, cultural historians; and a new cult of political determinism will take the place of economic determinism. For the moment, to be sure, there is still a touch of audacious heresy about any one who dares to question the infallibility of the economist's authority. But the time is not too far distant, perhaps, when the writer who attacks this same authority will be viewed, by all sensitive and humane persons, with as much disfavor as though he were clubbing a dead dog.

Yet, while the religion of Mammonism was with us, it might claim, as a distinction, that it offered a religious perspective the most meagre and the most ignominious of any faith that has ever imprisoned the human spirit. For it had no martyrology; and, as Ruskin pointed out, it could have none. But that it did have a clearly articulated metaphysics and theory of value can be seen at a glance by comparing Augustine with the classical economists that stem from Adam Smith. Just as for Augustine, it is God and His eternal will that govern the destinies of Christendom, so, for these economists, it is Nature and her eternal laws that ·preside over the destinies of the middle class. Just as Augustine thought of the state as an ancillary institution, to preserve peace and order, while the significant purposes of life were to be achieved in the church; so classical economics thinks of the state as an ancillary institution, to preserve peace and order, while the real values and meanings of life are to be found in economic enterprise. Here, indeed, we are still the inhabitants of Two Cities; only, we have substituted the City of Mammon for the City of God.

The more specific formulation of this theology for the Anglo-American democracies was achieved in the utilitarian succession of Bentham, Mill, and Spencer. Whoever has not read these philosophers has not properly understood the predominant mood of the British and the American peoples in recent generations. In Bentham we find a harsh orthodoxy, which lays down with legal precision the quota of pleasure and of pain, of profit and of loss, which, when balanced by the bookkeeper, goes to make up the meed of human happiness. In John Stuart Mill, there is an aristocratic regard for qualitative distinctions in pleasure and for the authority of the past, together with an appeal to the intuitive judgments of that newly won "sense of dignity" which a successful

middle class was now ready to substitute for rational cal-
culation. In Herbert Spencer, it is proved that pleasure-
giving—and profit-making—activities are also the life-
giving activities which make for the growth of the individual and of society; and there is accomplished a
final, "modernist" revision of the theology of Adam
Smith, in which it is shown not only that Mammonism
is compatible with Newtonian mechanics, but that its
triumphant destiny is written into the universal, all-
embracing law of evolution. With Jeremy Bentham, we
have a revolutionary middle class; with John Stuart
Mill, the middle classes have "arrived" on this
earth; with Herbert Spencer, the middle classes go to
heaven!

The great skeptic, David Hume, illustrates how
strong a hold this faith had on its partisans. Ordinarily,
Hume is held up as an example of that unrelenting intellectual honesty which is prepared to question the most
precious beliefs and the most sacred institutions. But he
never questioned the values of a bourgeois culture. In
his *Principles of Morals*, he talks complacently about our
"disinterested regard for riches"—this, apparently, his
substitute for Spinoza's "intellectual love of God!"—
and elaborates, in some detail, the "disagreeable images"
called up by the spectacle of poverty, and the "pleasing
ideas" evoked by the contemplation of wealth and of
plenty. His "model of perfect virtue" turns out to be a
business-man lawyer, who is equipped with a few more
of the aristocratic graces than Bentham would have

found necessary. And, in his discussion of the virtues, it is characteristic that he should take a fling at asceticism—*i.e.*, Christian ethics; should degrade the classical Greek virtues to the rank of the merely agreeable; should barely mention, and fail entirely to discuss, the "qualities useful to others;" and should make his longest list of virtues, under the heading of "qualities useful to ourselves," the traditional economic virtues of "discretion, caution, enterprise, industry, assiduity, frugality, economy, good-sense, prudence," and the like. Here, indeed, was a man who could doubt the identity of the self, the immortality of the soul, the truth of miracles, the scientific law of causality, and the existence of God, but who, not for one moment, entertained any doubt about the eternal validity of his middle class values.

The elaborate ritual needed to support this theology was worked out in some detail in the United States. The important act of "sacrifice," required to store up merit for the enjoyment of pleasures in a not too distant future, was the savings effected from one's hard-earned income. The holy book of which one contemplated the sacred symbols in a spirit of awe and of reverence was the account book. The daily devotional reading was the perusal of the stock market reports, while the weekly act of devotion was the deposit of one's "sacrifice" at the local bank, which had been designed in all the chaste beauty of a Greek temple. Pay-day took the place of Sunday as the appointed time for celebrating the goodness and power of the god Mammon. And, while not all the faithful should have the privilege of visiting the national shrine at Wall Street, they yet turned toward it in their moments of prayer and of aspiration, and made some contribution for the maintenance of its sanctuary in the hope that thus their local fields and factories might be blessed with increase of revenue.

It should not be thought, however, that the very rich—the "dirty capitalists"—were the most fervent worshipers at the temple of Mammon. They, indeed, had enough familiarity with this deity to know the definite limits of its Almighty Purchasing Power. The poor, also, were apt to be disillusioned of this religion, because they understood better than anyone else how much could be accomplished in life without its beneficent intervention. It was the middle classes that formed the stronghold of respectable piety—the classes that had just enough, and yet not quite enough—enough that they could savor the good things that came from the worship of Mammon, and yet not enough that they could discern the very real limitations of their presumably omnipotent God.

It is to be regretted that, in this bourgeois hedonism, there could not have been some of the aloofness of spirit that characterized the aristocratic hedonism of the Greeks. We are told of Aristippus, the Cyrenaic, that, once when he found himself on board a ship manned by pirates, he brought out his money under the pretense of counting it, and then, as though by accident, allowed it to fall overboard. When someone rebuked him for his carelessness, he replied: "It is better for the money to perish on account of Aristippus, than for Aristippus to perish on account of the money." But this superb detachment from the gifts of Mammon could hardly be achieved by the middle classes. Were there pirates abroad in the world, they would fain hold onto both their persons and their property. How, indeed, should a man part with his own soul!

That this worship of Mammon, with its glorification of pleasure and of profit, should blind men to the dimension of reason and of spirit in their make-up, needs no careful elaboration. But it brought with it other blindness, too. One of the items in the philosophy of Bentham most significant for us today is his attack on the "principle of asceticism," which he also called the "theological principle." As a hedonist, Bentham must hate pain, and so must be blind to the disciplinary rôle of pain and of suffering in the education of mankind. Accordingly, he makes these astounding remarks—which are a measure of a large part of the blindness of a bourgeois culture: that no one takes the "principle of asceticism" so seriously as to wish to inflict misery on others; and that this principle has never been made the law of any government. But was it never made the "law" of Sparta, or of Roman Stoicism, or of English and American Puritanism, or of Japanese Bushido, or of Nazi Germany? And for good and sufficient reason! As for the belief that no one can ever wish to inflict misery on others, this is part of the criminal fatuity of a bourgeois culture which cannot see that the punishment of the flesh may be a means for the discipline of the spirit; and which, also, looking upon the ravages of Japanese or of Nazi tyranny, can only shake its uncomprehending head in silly impotence, and cry, "No, no! These things cannot be!"

Desiring under no circumstances to be "a man of sorrows and acquainted with grief"—no Suffering Servant of the Lord for him!—the disciple of Mammon was hard put to it when faced with those conditions which called for a temper more heroic than hedonistic. Ages ago Aristotle had pointed out that the High-Minded Man will always prefer honor to profit, but this Middle-Minded Man had long taught himself that the honorable was the profitable. The horns of this dilemma gored cruelly the sensitive spirit of John Stuart Mill, who was utilitarian enough to believe in pleasure and in profit, and yet man enough to know that his destiny was to be something more than a well-fed pig. "Better to be a human being dissatisfied than a pig satisfied!" Yet how did the flesh yearn for the well-filled feed-bin and the warm mud-puddle of contented animality! Why must there be that better nature—or, rather, that nature not one's own—which called to a career more arduous and more sacrificial? Here, indeed, we have, in perfect type or symbol, that dreadful agony of soul which beset the Shylock peoples as they looked upon the marauder approaching their gates: My daughter! My ducats!— My honor! My profits!—My freedom! My comfort!— Who shall deliver me from this body of torments?

The sentimentalism inherent in this whole outlook should not be hard to discern. For what is sentimentalism, if it be not the easy exercise of human functions below the level of rational discipline and of spiritual delight of which they are susceptible? Sentimentalism in love is love that rests content with all that is cheap and facile in the affections, and which has no glimpse of the dimension of sacrificial devotion or of the comradeship of true minds. Surely, then, any philosophy which made of man a mere body, a mere collection of sensations and impressions, a mere machine for calculating pleasure and pain, profit and loss—without any questing intellect, or any aspiring soul—surely this was the grossest sentimentalism!

The sentimentalism of the British had an advantage over American sentimentalism only in that a traditional reserve of manner compelled it to find outlet in modes more subtle and more refined. But the evidences of this sentimentalism were everywhere in a bourgeois culture. It showed itself in a modern educational program which refused to regard children any longer as potential adults, or as potential sons and daughters of God, but encouraged, with loving folly, the most infantile of their impulses and the most unproductive of their responses. At the same time, it put more stress on calories and vitamins than on character, emphasized "socialization" rather than individual discipline, and looked with horror on any premature effort to evoke in the child those first stirrings of mind and of soul which might serve it so well later on. Its pet abomination was the arbitrary discipline of a previous generation, so it sought to abolish all discipline. Because it understood the body better than the mind, it reveled in righteous indignation over the brutality of the old form of physical punishment—the cries of physical pain are overt and therefore "real"—while, through lack of discipline, it gave the child a sense of moral insecurity and of spiritual uncertainty that was the more cruelly hurtful to the degree that it could not be objectively noted.

This same sentimentalism was manifest in the popular pacifism of recent decades. How loud it was in its outcries against the terrible loss of life in war! And how blind it was to the moral degradation of tyranny—the destruction of liberties, the abolition of the rights of conscience, the breaking of the spirit of once-free peoples, the pride and arrogance bred in the conqueror, the obliteration of all the cherished values of a hard-won civilization. It is not to be denied that war also brings moral degradation. But when one sets five or six years of the moral degradation of war against fifty, or a hundred —I do not say a thousand—years of the total degradation of a Nazi or a Japanese tyranny, then should a man made in the image of a just God hesitate in his decision? The popular pacifist could not receive that hard saying —to fear not that which kills the body, but, rather, to fear that which is able to destroy both body and soul in hell. And is not tyranny such a destroyer?—Nay, rather, let us live—if not with honor, then without honor! As for the soul, there is none! All we know here is the body!

On a more pedestrian plane, the mood of sentimentalism revealed itself as a regressive yearning for "frankness" in all human affairs, and in a detestation of all "hypocrisy."—The hypocrite and the idealist, are they not one? But look at us: we are not idealists, and therefore not hypocrites: in all matters, frank and openhanded—frankly animals—that is our honesty!—But hypocrisy is the high privilege of a spiritual being. Should man cease to be a hypocrite, he would cease to be human. The pagan, animal man has not in him enough of aspiration or of imagination to play the hypocrite. On the other hand, the Pharisee, the unwitting hypocrite, is one who believes that his ideals are already the reality of his character. Most of us, it is hoped, are witting hypocrites, aware of the discrepancy between what we are and what we should be, occasionally pretending to be what we are not, but at least knowing enough in our hypocrisy to be ashamed of what is base in ourselves, to curb now and then an overt act of bestiality, and to point the direction of our effort toward the ideal.

But the age of Mammon—"this lubrique and adult-'rate age"—cared not for even a witting hypocrisy, as it cared neither for reason nor for spirit. Its attitude toward all out-reachings of the soul to a higher destiny is fittingly symbolized in the posture of a certain character portrayed in *The Clouds* of Aristophanes. The old man, Strepsiades, is visiting the Thinkery, in order to learn from the sophists some new device for outwitting his creditors. Around him there squat, or prance, various figures which illustrate the branches of human learning. One figure is bent down from the waist, with his buttocks thrust heavenward, and with his nose buried deep in the ground. "And what is that fellow studying?" queries Strepsiades. "He's examining the bowels of the earth," answers the guide. "But that buttocks of his—what is it doing up in the air?" "Ah, that's studying astronomy all by itself!" Likewise, the Man of Mammon has had his mind's eye glued to the material advantages of existence, and has lent but the tail-end of his intellect to the contemplation of affairs celestial.

### III

This blindness of the modern man was a learned blindness—a *docta ignorantia*. After a preliminary purification in the "science of economics" and in the mechanistic "science of psychology," and after a few seasons of pure sentimental contemplation, he was ready for that intuitive moment of mysticism in which one stands face to face with the beatific vision, and all the categories of common sense fall away. For this "learned ignorance" was most blind to those simple realities which, to the unsophisticated man, stand forth in clearest outline. It could no longer make the most elementary ethical judgments. It could not understand others, because it could not understand itself. It no longer knew the meaning either of man as an individual, or of man as a member of society.

Henry Ford is an excellent epitome of this condition. Without question he is one of the greatest industrial and mechanical geniuses of this generation. It is also true that few men have been so blind to the social realities of the world in which they lived. He could startle other manufacturers by being one of the first to pay high wages to labor: that was sound economics. But he never quite understood the laboring man as a human being; and so, when, in recent times, the treatment of labor became a broadly social rather than a narrowly economic question, he proved to be one of the most recalcitrant of employers. He understood man as a consumer well enough to envision the miracle that could be wrought in American rural life with the model "T" Ford, but his inability to grasp the full cultural implications of the machine is mirrored in his nostalgic turning to the arts and handicrafts of a pre-industrial era. In the Second World War —perhaps with the prompting of his son Edsel—he was a shrewd enough industrialist and good enough patriot to pour his energies into the production of tanks and of airplanes; but he was more true to his social philosophy when, in the First World War, he outfitted a Peace Ship, and sent his missionaries over to persuade the Kaiser and Lloyd George that they really had nothing to fight about after all. History is bunk! human nature is bunk!—But money and machinery: these are real!

The tragic figure of Charles Lindbergh illustrates the

same dilemma. Undoubtedly he had his own good personal reasons for being disillusioned with human emotions and with popular passions. But this simply confirmed him in an initial bias which was sympathetic to the machine, but which could not comprehend the men that made it and used it. The latent fascism in his prewar discourses was all the more significant because Lindbergh himself never recognized its character. With him, it was simply an intuitive preference for a social order which should be stripped of the irrelevancies of human freedom and of human feeling, and which should display only the cold, steely precision of a beautifully-tuned airplane motor. Even when he visited Germany and marveled at the industrial might of its war machine, he never understood the religious passion, the human sacrifices, and the creative frenzy which built that machine. Indeed, if he had seen Germany before the rise of the Nazi party, he would probably have said to Hitler then what, later, he said to the United States—that no nation so lacking in the industrial sinews of war could possibly hope to stand up to an enemy on the field of battle. Machinery?—that is something tangible and real. Morale?—one doesn't quite know about that. And yet this deep ethical blindness was found in a man who, in terms of physical and moral courage and of high sincerity, was himself one of the finest representatives of a tradition that we like to think is American.

One found this same incredible blindness in American visitors to foreign countries. The tourist in China could

not see through the material differences between Chinese
culture and our own to the underlying spiritual affinities.
He noted the backward state of industry and of agricul-
ture, the lack of hygiene and of sanitation, the primitive
character of transportation, the paucity of bath-tubs and
of motion picture emporiums, and the high price of
chewing-gum and of razor-blades. He did not see: that,
in spite of war-lords, the Chinese, like ourselves, were an
essentially peaceful folk devoted to the pursuits of commerce; that they were practising an ancient *laissez-faire*
and local autonomy in business and in politics that ante-
dated by centuries our own theorists of free enterprise
and of democracy; that, like ourselves, their loyalty to
the family and to the community took precedence—almost too much—over their loyalty to the state; that
their real aristocracy was the only kind that can be tolerated in a democracy—the aristocracy of education and
of talent. To such an observer, it was Japan that was the
true spiritual kin of the United States. Such zeal for the
latest industrial techniques! Such Yankee ingenuity in
imitation and in invention! Such splendid newspapers
and such wide-spread literacy! Now, there was progress
for you!

The obverse of our blindness toward China was
shown, not only in our blindness toward Japan, but in
our blindness toward Nazi Germany. In the two latter
instances, it was the inability to see through material resemblances to fundamental spiritual differences. The
American traveler in Germany was impressed by mag-

nificent *auto-bahnen*, by great industries a-building, by
the brilliant applications of technology, by the discipline,
order, cleanliness, decency, and contentedness of the
common folk. Here was that efficiency expert's paradise
which somehow even the nation that fathered behavior-
istic psychology had never quite been able to impose on
itself. Everything so well adjusted—no loose ends, no
labor troubles, no unemployment, no incompetent police! Perhaps, then, Adolf Hitler was a gravely misunderstood man. Had he not bettered the condition of
his people? Had he not taught them joy in work, as well
as strength through joy? As for those Jews—perhaps
the Nazis were right;—and they probably had it coming
to them, anyway!—And so, because the outside of the
platter was clean, one did not see that within it was full
of extortion and excess.

But the attitude of the Anglo-American peoples toward Russia was a confusion twice compounded of the
inability to distinguish between fact and theory, and between material reality and spiritual reality. Taken as
rigid and exclusive orthodoxies, both capitalism and
communism are branches of the worship of Mammon.
Taken as historical processes and as liberal faiths, they
are both efforts to approximate some ideal kingdom of
ends. Consequently, we witness the bizarre situation that
either capitalist, or communist, in the mood of sober
realism, declares himself to be a hard-headed materialist; and that either one, in the mood of high idealism and
of righteous indignation, denounces the other for being

a crass materialist. There is truth and there is falsity in both statements. And, if the two sects belabor one another with such ferocity, it is because they are, after all, but two separate denominations of a common faith which, from a Christian perspective, have more resemblances between them than they have differences. The confusion can be cleared up only by noting first the actual mind-set of the Russian people and of the Anglo-American peoples, and then, as another task, by scrutinizing the formal creeds of capitalism and of communism.

If ever, as a purely descriptive statement, we remarked that the Russians were materialists, we erred. On the contrary, in point of fact, we were the materialists, while the Russians were the idealists. Harry Ward once expressed it by saying that these two parties were like the two sons whose father bade them go work in the vineyard: the Russian son said, I will not, but he went; the Anglo-American son said, I will, but he went not. The difference between them may also be expressed by saying that it is the difference between the first generation of materialists and the second generation of materialists. The first generation of materialists—the Russian communists, or the "Robber Barons" of the pioneering phase of American economic history—have in them a certain zest for the game, a certain delight in the struggle for its own sake, an unduly exalted vision of the wonderful rewards of conquest, that enable them to make sacrifices and to undergo risks that are seemingly incommensurate with the purely material reward they seek. They are disciples of Mammon whose possession of a primitive *élan vital* endows them with a certain aura of idealism, and rescues them from complete subservience to the god whom they officially worship. But the second generation of materialists—the Anglo-American peoples—is already enjoying the outcome of the hard effort of its forebears. These folk are so enamored of the physical comforts they possess, that they have actually forgotten at what a price these comforts were bought. They are disciples of Mammon who live parasitically in the court of the temple, and no longer labor in the field to bring in the first fruits of their vineyards and herds and flocks. These are the real materialists.

Yet considered as formal creeds, both capitalism and communism illustrate the ethical blindness of materialism. The communist extols an ideal class-less society of justice, and peace, and brotherhood. Yet the man whom he summons to sacrifice for this goal is, by him, described as a bare reflex of the environment, a mere automaton of economic forces, who, by definition, is neither worth the sacrifice to be made, nor able to make it himself. The communist, moreover, identifies his opponent with a property system, and is unable to see aught that spills over. Too often he forgets that most of his distinguished leaders came, not from the proletariat, but from the despised class of bourgeois intellectuals. In damning the individual capitalist, he cheats himself of the opportunity of learning what the capitalist can tell him better than anyone else—namely, the limited satisfactions that go with purely economic resources. And, in damning the capitalist system for its inequitable *laissez-faire*, he is ready to dispose of the civil and religious liberties that appeared along with economic liberty.

The capitalist suffers from a similar obliquity of vision. Officially he thinks of himself as a mere machine for accumulating profits. Even though he may be keenly sensitive to the multifarious interests of a complex society, and even though his own private impulses may lead him far astray from the straight and narrow path, he feels obliged, at least in public, always to maintain that the profit-motive is the sole foundation and cement of society. Moreover, his opinion of the laboring man is as degraded as his opinion of himself. He thinks of labor as a commodity to be bought on the market like any other economic goods and services. But labor is not a commodity. Labor is human beings. And so the capitalist is haunted by weird nightmares of an organized uprising of commodities, the liquidating of the owners of industry, the socializing of all the instruments of production, and, perhaps, the election of John L. Lewis as president of the Congress of Industrial Commodities of the United States.

That Mammonism should have had its own internally divisive factions is simply proof of the scope and vitality of the religion, and that it should have been unable to see the common denominator in these sects is evidence of its inability to rise to a plane of reason and of spirit beyond its own scheme of values. The purblind character of this perspective, however, shows itself most dramatically in the interpretation of the individual. For, in decadent second-generation capitalism, as in orthodox communism, there are no individuals: there are only corporations, classes, economic forces, externally motivated robots. Among the Anglo-American peoples, then, this religion could no longer discern its own "heroes," nor read aright its own enemies.

It was precisely the materialistic rendering of human motives that blinded us so long to the real character of the drives and ambitions of an Adolf Hitler. The more we "explained" him on economic grounds, the less we understood what he was all about, and the easier it was for him to pull more wool over our already dim eyes. For Hitler belongs to a dimension of conduct which is clear beyond the ignoble bourgeois calculus of pleasure and pain, of profit and loss. A frankly ethical interpretation would have seen him at once for just what he is—a menacing embodiment of the Nietzschean Will-to-Power. It would have placed him immediately in the great and terrible tradition of an Alexander, a Genghis Khan, an Attila, a Napoleon Bonaparte; and it would have known that only one thing could satisfy him finally —and that is what satisfies God—namely, the Kingdom, and the Power, and the Glory!

In the comprehension of its own "heroes," this bourgeois culture was equally myopic. It is true that, when the American people had a Coolidge for president, they sensed somehow that here was a pure embodiment of the most chaste ideal of Mammonism. And yet the public never really understood of what sort was this "hero": —this Yankee Mahatma—this Republican *roi-fainéant* —this great American apostle of *wu-wei!*—incorruptible in his complacency, smug to the point of sublimity! —fit symbol, this, for a generation spiritually steatopygous, of which the mummy, should it be by some curious antiquarian in future time exhumed, shall be pronounced more noteworthy for the prominence of its ischial callosities than for any tokens of achievement moral or intellectual!

Nor was British Mammonism without its avatar. Good old Nev!—this John Bull strangely metamorphosed into Ferdinand the Bull. How did he love all green pastures and still waters! 'Spite of banderilleros, and picadors, and matadors, fain would he have peace— and prosperity—in our time. Yet even in the shade beneath the old oak in his back-yard intrudes the sting of the bumble-bee!

The difference between a Coolidge and a Chamberlain is worth noting. It is the difference between complacency and complaisance; between a younger man and an older man; between a younger civilization and an older civilization; between prosperity and peril. In Coolidge there is reflected the superb smugness of a youthful culture, secure in the enjoyment of all good things, and made invincible, by ignorance, against the slightest intimation of impending disaster. In Chamberlain, there is a doting smugness—eager, in spite of it all, to find occasions to please, and finding them; more aware, in its maturity, of the dangers that beset one, yet ready to believe that, with some little adjustment, everything will be all right in the end. Each of these men, in his own way, however, symbolized the dry rot in a bourgeois culture; and neither one could really see the catastrophe toward which this generation marched any more than could the people they governed.

Blind fools that lead the blind! And if the blind lead the blind, shall they not both fall into the ditch?

But perhaps we should pause to erect a more fitting memorial to these "heroes" of a day that is gone. And perhaps we should not speak too ill of the ripe civilization that gave them birth. *De mortuis nil nisi bonum!* After all, they were the fair flower of the compost of materialism, hedonism, and sentimentalism. And, just as it took generations of Hebrew suffering, and exile, and sinfulness, and sacrifice, to prepare the way for the divinely begotten Son of God, so did it take generations of the Anglo-American flesh-pots of fatness and of ease to prepare the way for the coming of these two Sons of Mammon.

IV

It was part of the blindness of this age, that it should turn to the worship of false gods which might claim more magical powers than could the very tangible Baals before which it also bowed down. For, even when man officially denies his spiritual destiny, he cannot altogether still those promptings of mind and of soul which reach out for a higher meaning. These false gods were a projection of the spiritual pellagra of the times. They were a curious compound of some of the insights of the great historic traditions in science and in religion with the fundamental mood of the prevailing Mammonism.

The backwash of the First World War cast forth two of these faiths. One of them was Dialectical Theology, which, as it was formulated in Europe, and partly adopted in the United States, was initially an expression of disillusionment with modern materialism, but which, in final structure, simply aped the new Satanism of the fascist creed. It substituted religious absolutism for political and economic absolutism, religious myth for racial myth, theological obscurantism for nationalistic mysticism, and an anti-historical god for a trans-empirical state. In its writings one found the same messianic emotionalism as in the speeches of the new Nazi führer— urgent, repetitious, ponderous, categorically damning, and without reason redeeming. This was Hitlerism in theology. And there was precious little about it that was even dialectical until Reinhold Niebuhr wedded it to the social pragmatism of his native American heritage.

Dialectical Theology was only for the religionists. Its counterpart, Positivism, was only for the philosophers. If the religionists went on a binge of beliefulness, then the philosophers must try a diet of skepticism. For Positivism was the queasy-stomached valetudinarian in philosophy—endlessly counting its calories and tabulating its vitamins: a sort of intellectual dyspepsia exalted into a metaphysic and a method—forever fearful lest, by permitting ingestion to the meaningless phantasmagorias of speculative thought, it stuff itself to death; when, to all that beheld it objectively, its final end was only too clear, namely, that it must starve itself to death! For all the world like a belly-bloated victim of famine, now in a state of hallucination, who, beholding the inflated condition of his abdomen, should imagine that his difficulty was that he had been eating too much!

Dialectical Theology, a wind-bellows! Positivism, a cathartic! To be blown up mightily—with wind; and, again, to be purged mightily—of wind: these were the alternatives offered to a spiritually famished generation. Both doctrines reflect the post-war failure of nerve: the one, a shrill, screaming summons to a transcendent realm of value; the other, a retreat to the secure shell of logical and scientific certitude. Both appeal to authority: the one cannot integrate its authority with historical fact; the other cannot integrate its authority with abiding value. Both seek the Absolute: the one wants its Absolute whole; the other wants the Absolute broken up into little bits. Both claim to be strong medicine for the urgent needs of the time. Strong medicine, indeed, for the weak and the defeated who can no longer stomach the rich bread of life!

From a different quarter comes the pseudo-Hindu mysticism of Aldous Huxley and of Gerald Heard. In Huxley this has its significance in that it originates from the Freudian phallic worship, so prevalent for a decade after the First World War, and now reflects the disillusionment which any civilized man must feel with the adoration of the flesh. No one in our time has drawn, with such *saeva indignatio* as has Huxley, the portrait of the purely animal man and of the purely mechanical man; and his *Brave New World* may well come to rank with the great classics in the literature of satire.

But, just as when Huxley worshiped the flesh, he could not blend into it the spirit; so, when he worships the spirit, he cannot find its organic union with the flesh. The result is a dualism. One half of us exists on an animal level, where the good is the proper functioning of the organism in accord with the laws of its own being. The other half exists on a level where individuality is obliterated into an impersonal, spiritual, ultimate reality, and where we may practise the disinterested virtues of "non-attachment" without desire and without aversion. And so, as in Hinduism, beneath the rising arc of spiritual pretension, one discerns the undercurrent of carnality, of pessimism, cynicism, egotism, of the evil fascination of the flesh which one yet lusts after even as he holds it in contempt. The stages of conversion to this faith are stereotyped: first, a pagan delight in the joys of the flesh; next, the fierce revolt of mind and of soul against the merely animal in man; and, finally, the turning toward an idealism which is as emasculated as the original paganism was despiritualized. Here, indeed, is the invariable pattern of the rake's progress toward religion. Its mature dogma has already found classic formulation in Schopenhauer. Only a Greek fever germ saved Lord Byron from becoming a convert.

*The Third Morality* of Gerald Heard provides a more ladylike version of the same faith. Here, at last, we have superseded the interim ethic of the Sermon on the Mount, and there is revealed to us the ultimate truth in religion! In place of the old monastic disciplines of chastity, poverty, and obedience, we are warned to rid ourselves of physical addiction, of possessiveness, and of pretensions. Vegetarianism and kindness to animals are greatly extolled. We are to handle all life by the method of pure good will. Even snakes, it is said, respond to music; and we must believe that the large carnivora can, with patience, be tamed—(thus, even Hitler?). War is one of the greatest of evils, because it inflames individuality; and also because, no doubt, it calls for too high a protein-intake for the fighting man. Mid much discussion of problems of euthanasia, breathing exercises, good posture, contraception, tea *vs.* alcohol, abortion, and suicide, there is also some word in favor of "compassion." Yet one deplores any materialistic humanitarianism; and there is never mention made of anything so vulgar as self-sacrificial love. Like Huxley, Gerald Heard gives considerable attention to sexual matters. Quite on his own account, he intimates that, among the people of the future, the adolescent, homosexual phase of sex will play an increasingly important rôle. Unlike Huxley, he believes that training in the physical tenderness of sex may be a preparation for spiritual tenderness.

Yet Jesus knew nothing of the physical tenderness of

sex. Saint Francis knew nothing of it. Abraham Lincoln probably knew nothing of it. And the literature of the Casanovas and Don Juans is ample evidence that one may be a master of all the arts of physical tenderness and yet never rise to the plane of spiritual tenderness. Indeed, to believe that there is a necessary and simple transition from the love of woman to the love of humanity, or to the love of God, is part of the gross sentimentalism of a materialistic age. Gerald Heard, with his pale piety and emaciated mysticism, is the perfect spokesman of this mood. But between his Hindu "compassion" and Christian "love" there is as much difference as between the wearied spirituality of the *Meditations* of, Marcus Aurelius and the dynamic energy of the early apostles and martyrs of the church. To be able to discern this difference is almost the touchstone of good taste in religion. The fact that, in our day, this diluted doctrine should have been welcomed by some Christians as ancillary to their own faith must be taken as evidence, either of an excess of open-minded tolerance, or of our passing once more through one of those decadent phases in which it is believed that a pernicious anemia of the spirit is the first precondition to salvation.

However, the noblest achievement of the Age of Mammon in its blind quest for spiritual fulfillment was pacifism. I do not refer, of course, to the disciplined pacifism of an historic tradition like that of the Quakers —for which pacifism, indeed, is too pale and too cold a term. But I do refer to that widespread popular pacifism which Reinhold Niebuhr has rightly characterized as an unholy compound of Christian perfectionism and of bourgeois love of ease. What had happened was that a materialistic civilization had grown old. In spite of much silly talk about a "predatory, imperialistic capitalism," the fact was that capitalism was no longer a beast of prey. To accuse it of greed and rapacity was to flatter it with the possession of a vitality which it had not known for many years. Already this great beast had clipped its own tail, gold-tipped its horns, sheathed its claws in silver like a mandarin's, run a ring through its nose for the use of a master, and now, weary of striving, sated with animal satisfactions, sunk in sloth and ease, lay, in helpless obesity, contemplating with mystical rapture the global fullness of its rotund belly, and desiring but one thing above all other things—that it be left in peace!

v

The blind man yet sits by the wayside, begging. For the eye is the light of the soul; and, if that light be darkened, then how great is the darkness!

But whether this blind man, with Pharisaic complacency, believing that he can see as well as another, should beg, not for light, but for more jewels and for more garments to cover his already pampered body, that were one thing.

But it were another thing, if, knowing his blindness, he should beg:

"Lord, that I may receive my sight!"

# Two

# THE HIDDEN
# TALENT

*For the kingdom of heaven is as a man travelling into a far country, who called his own servants, and delivered unto them his goods. And unto one he gave five talents, to another two, and to another one; to every man according to his several ability; and straightway took his journey.*

*Then he that had received the five talents went and traded with the same, and made them other five talents. And likewise he that had received two, he also gained other two. But he that had received one went and digged in the earth, and hid his lord's money.*

*After a long time the lord of those servants cometh, and reckoneth with them.*

*And so he that had received five talents came and brought other five talents, saying, Lord, thou deliveredst unto me five talents: behold, I have gained beside them five talents more. His lord said unto him, Well done, thou good and faithful servant: thou hast been faithful over a few things, I will make thee ruler over many things: enter thou into the joy of thy lord. He also that had received two talents came and said, Lord, thou deliveredst unto me two talents: behold, I have gained two other talents beside them. His lord said unto him, Well done, good and faithful servant; Thou hast been faithful over a few things, I will make thee ruler over many things: enter thou into the joy of thy lord.*

*Then he which had received the one talent came and said, Lord, I knew thee that thou art an hard man, reaping where thou hast not sown, and gathering where thou hast not strawed: And I was afraid, and went and hid thy talent in the earth: lo, there thou hast that is thine.*

*His lord answered and said unto him, Thou wicked and slothful servant, thou knewest that I reap where I sowed not, and gather where I have not strawed: Thou oughtest therefore to have put my money to the exchangers, and then at my coming I should have received mine own with usury. Take therefore the talent from him, and give it unto him which hath ten talents. For unto every one that hath shall be given, and he shall have abundance: but from him that hath not shall be taken away even that which he hath. And cast ye the unprofitable servant into outer darkness: there shall be weeping and gnashing of teeth.*

*Matthew 25:14–30.*

# 2:

## THE HIDDEN
## TALENT

ONE of the earliest isolationists reported in literature was the wicked and slothful servant who went and hid his talent in a field. The talent was not his own. It had been entrusted to him by his Lord. Unfortunately this Lord was notorious for the genial *laissez-faire* with which he ran his estate. It appears that he liked, when possible, to have people exercise their individual initiative. He had a rather idealistic faith that, if they were left to their own devices, their common sense would enable them to profit from their experience. So it was that he neglected to tell this servant what to do with the talent.

Now, it should not be thought that this servant was altogether such a bad sort of fellow as the story would have it. On the contrary, he was an eminently respectable chap, who had achieved quite a reputation in the community for strictly minding his own business, and for never meddling in the affairs of others. Consequently, when the talent was put in his care, he very naturally decided to keep it in a place apart, just as he had always done with his own person. To be sure, if he put the talent

out to trade, or left it with the exchangers, it might yield
some usury; and, at the end, he would probably have
two talents instead of one. But, also, what he would have
then would be somewhat soiled by passing from the
hands of one man to another. It would not be the original talent, all spick-and-span, the way it had been delivered to him, and the way he hoped to return it. So he
went and digged in the earth, and hid his Lord's money.

The coming again of the Lord brought quite a shock
to the respectable servant. Far from appreciating the
care that had been taken to preserve the original talent
in all its purity, the Lord seemed to think it would be
much better to have a few more talents on hand by now,
even though they weren't identical with the first one, and
even though they were a bit soiled by circulation. So the
Lord called him a wicked and slothful servant. More
than that, the Lord took away the talent, and gave it to
another servant who already had ten talents. One would
think that was punishment enough—with just a touch of
vindictiveness, too. But the Lord, who could get pretty
mad at times, went even farther than that. He ordered
the unprofitable servant to be cast into outer darkness,
where there should be weeping and wailing and gnashing of teeth.

The heirs of the wicked and slothful servant have
been many on the earth, and they bear witness that they
are the sons of their father. They have expounded systems of philosophy, founded religious sects, proclaimed
moral laws, developed theories of art, and controlled

American foreign policy. As philosophers, they have taught that ultimate reality is something too pure and too chaste to be polluted by incarnation in the course of historical events and characters. As religionists, they have cut themselves off from the corruption of the body politic, and have walked their own way with gingerly held petticoats lest they be spattered by mud. As ethicists, they have extolled principles so immutable and so transcendent as to be exempt from the degrading, empirical test of consequences in conduct. As aestheticians, they have placed art first, and said that we must cultivate art only for the sake of art. As politicians in the United States, they have placed America first, and have trumpeted that we must use America only for the sake of Americans.

Political isolationism, aesthetic isolationism, moral isolationism, religious isolationism, philosophical isolationism: they are all one. Each conceives that its peculiar talent is something so precious that it dare not be put out to circulate in the hands of men, but must be hid in a field, or laid up on a shelf, in magnificent immunity from all fruitful interaction with the rest of life. Each makes the discovery, too late, that what is hid in the closet is consumed by the moth, that what is buried in the field is corrupted by the rust, and that only those talents persevere in their lustre which brave the light of day and the marts of men. Not only, then, does each fail to gain new talents, but there is taken away from him even that which he had.

II

There is a passage in the sixth book of Plato's *Republic*
which is worth quoting in its entirety, because it gives a
classic statement of the isolationist mood, and also, perhaps, because it illustrates how, in an ampler age, men
could express their prejudices with a more diffuse ele-
gance than can we in the vulgar hurry of this day:

"Now he who has become a member of this little
band, and has tasted how sweet and blessed his treasure
is, and has watched the madness of the many, with the
full assurance that there is scarcely a person who takes a
single judicious step in his public life, and that there is
no ally with whom he may safely march to the succour
of the just; nay, that, should he attempt it, he will be
like a man that has fallen among wild beasts—unwilling
to join in their iniquities, and unable singly to resist the
fury of all, and therefore destined to perish before he
can be of any service to his country or his friends, and to
do no good to himself or any one else; having, I say,
weighed all this, such a man keeps quiet and confines
himself to his own concerns, like one who takes shelter
behind a wall on a stormy day, when the wind is driving
before it a hurricane of dust and rain; and when from
his retreat he sees the infection of lawlessness spreading
over the rest of mankind, he is well content, if he can in
any way live his life here untainted in his own person by
unrighteousness and unholy deeds, and, when the time

for his release arrives, take his departure amid bright hopes with cheerfulness and serenity." *

Here we have all the essential features of the doctrine: the little band of the elect, with its blessed treasure, scrupulously minding its own concerns; the storm, and the sheltering wall; the madness of the many, the wild beasts without, the infection of lawlessness spreading over mankind; and the exclusive concern for personal salvation, regardless of the unredeemed state of society.

It is interesting to note that Plato was not at the beginning an isolationist. The early dialogues reveal a thinker who was concerned with practical problems of statesmanship: how to find a secure basis for morality; how to transmit ethical wisdom from one generation to the next; how to work out an intelligent educational program; how to place men of ability in the offices of government; how to plan a just and an effectively functioning state. The fact that, in spite of repeated discouragement, he made three separate visits to Syracuse in an effort to convert the tyrant into a philosopher-king is evidence of his stubborn persistence in a practical program. But the first visit ended with his being sold into slavery; the second was followed by a premature sabbatical leave; and the third ended in imprisonment. The result, temporarily, at least, was disillusionment with the possibility of translating his ideals into working realities. And so Plato became an isolationist. The natural functioning of a compensatory mechan-

* From Plato, *Republic*, Davies & Vaughan trs., 1921, p. 214. By permission of The Macmillan Company, publishers.

ism then helped him to conclude that the majority of men were sunk in a brutish animality, that philosophy was too choice a pearl to be cast before swine, and that the true sage must learn to retire behind the walls of his academy and be content "if he can in any way live his life here untainted in his own person by unrighteousness and unholy deeds."

The attitude of Plato in the passage just quoted is too often characteristic of the classical Greek philosophers. This attitude, moreover, provides an instructive contrast with the mood that was typical of Sparta. For just as the Athenian Greek sought to isolate the intellect, so did the Spartan seek to isolate the body. One finds something of the Spartan position in the dialogue *Laches*. Two generals are discussing the problem of military training. Nicias, a tactician, wishes to teach his men the arts of strategy. Laches, a blunt warrior and a man of action, cares only for the forthright fighting methods of the Lacedaemonians. He is afraid that, if his men rely too much on intelligence, they will neglect the discipline of their bodies, and that a man who is clever at tactics will too easily find excuses for playing the coward. The antithesis is between strength of body and of character, on the one hand, and shrewdness and ingenuity of mind, on the other. In a rough way, it is the antithesis between Athenian culture and Spartan culture. Each selected a prized value and tried to isolate it from contaminating contact with the rest of life. Just how far the classical Greeks meant to go in their isolation of the intellect can be read in the sixth book of Plato's *Republic* and in the tenth book of Aristotle's *Nicomachean Ethics*.

The isolation from one another of two values which, in this instance, took place in distinct cultures, has, for the American scene, long been a part of a single tradition. For over fifty years, now, John Dewey has been complaining of the divorce between theory and practice in the *mores* of the American people. One half of this divorce goes back to a pioneer tradition which valued physical hardihood and strength of character, and which tended to regard all theory and book larnin' as useless academic impedimenta that were irrelevant to the significant functions of life. The other half goes back to a genteel tradition which deliberately accentuated the otiose and non-utilitarian character of its "culture." The thorough-going manner in which this divorce between theory and practice was long maintained was highlighted by the tremendous clamor that arose when the New Deal initiated the "brain trust" in government, and began, openly and unashamedly, to employ university-trained men in the ordinary offices of state. To many an American purist this was almost as indecent as the conjunction of an angel and an animal.

Another interesting polarity in the mood of isolationism lies between the medieval ascetic and the modern sexationalist. The prized value of the ascetic was spirit; and, in order to have it pure and undefiled, he fled from the evil ways of society, with its allurements of the flesh, its temptations to avarice and acquisitiveness, and all its occasions for prideful ambition, and retired to some desert place where, it was presumed, he might possess his soul in peace. The dilettante in love, on the other hand, was eager to extract from sex every least drop of sensuous pleasure, so cut himself off as carefully as could be from any possibility of a spiritual union which might distract his attention from the more tangible value.

Again, to speak of art for art's sake in the same breath as one talks of America for the Americans is at least as illuminating as it is ludicrous. Art for art's sake developed as a cult at a time when the artist had lost his sense of organic union with the rest of society. It was never a cult in any great creative period, like that of the Renaissance or of classical Greece, when the artist took it for granted that his work must fuse with the other functions of a richly diversified civilization. When it was pursued as a cult, the initial effect might be some refinement of techniques, the discovery of a few new resources, and, perhaps, two or three bold experiments in an unconventional direction. But the final outcome was meaninglessness, incoherence, and sterility. The moral for politics is precisely the same as the moral for aesthetics.

With a few exceptions, the aetiology of these cases is pretty much the same: first of all, an inadequately based idealism, followed by disillusionment, and then isolation, and compensation. American isolationism was at its strongest after the frustrations of the First World War. The spiritual isolationism of the ascetic gained fresh intensity from the fall of the Roman Empire—an event

which helped to convince him that this earth was no place
for the building of an ideal order, and that all he could
hope to do was to prepare himself, by strict discipline,
for citizenship in the kingdom of another world. The
disciple of Freud and of D. H. Lawrence was disillusioned with the cruelty and hypocrisy which appeared to
result from the Victorian effort to idealize love and to
make it respectable, so he tried to discover the richer
meanings of sex in an unabashed animality which was
tormented by no qualms of reason or of conscience. The
American frontiersman had, as part of his cultural heritage, a recollection of the polished incompetence in practical affairs of the scholar; so he wished to enjoy his
newly found freedom, inventive ingenuity, and opportunity for self-expression, unhampered by the elegant
inanities of the higher learning. And the American
scholar, unless he had in him some of the tough pragmatism of his own people, must have become increasingly
aware that the aristocratic, leisured tradition of which he
was the bearer had little relevance, for the moment, to
the problems of this great, broad, bawdy, dynamic democracy.

The consequences of isolationism also display a strik-
ing uniformity. It is found in the one-sided development
of the value isolated—a failure to realize its full potentialities. The classical Greek thinker, in his isolation of
the intellect, disdained the manual arts and crafts, and
so failed to develop an experimental science. Similarly,
the early American scholar, cherishing the gentility of

his calling, failed for long to integrate his learning with the technology and the practical skills that were really building his country. The tradition of the American pioneer, with its distrust of theory, survived both in business and in political practice with the result that these two areas remained unilluminated by intelligence for many years of our history. The Spartan warrior and athlete might glorify the body, but, because he did not see the relationship of the body to higher levels of activity, he was unable to celebrate its grace and strength in enduring art forms which might inspire later generations. The medieval anchorite wished to keep his soul pure from the world, but too often the result was impurity of soul, and, in any case, a failure to achieve that well-tempered spirituality which a Jesus and a Saint Francis found by living in the world of men. Likewise, it may be said of the sensualist, quite simply, that a chief defect of his program is that he fails to get out of sex all that can be got out of it.

So it is that isolationism defeats itself.


III

It is significant that the great religions of the world have not succumbed to the isolationist temper. This is as true of the secular religions of democracy, nationalism, fascism, and communism, as it is of Christianity, Buddhism, and Mohammedanism. They did not hide their talent in a field, but put it out to trade, so that where there had been one talent there should now be other talents.

It was, indeed, a critical moment in history when Saint Paul confronted those who wished to make of Christianity merely another sect within Judaism. Like all conservatives, these spiritual isolationists had too great a regard for the historic sources of their doctrine and too little confidence in its future. They appreciated the strength that came to Christianity from its connection with the ancient discipline of the Hebrew people, but they were of such little faith as to doubt that the seed of their religion could strike root in an alien culture and still bloom with characteristic beauty. They were afraid for what might be lost, and could not see what might be gained. Saint Paul had vision enough to perceive that what would be lost was the trivial and the irrelevant, and that what would be gained was a purifying and strengthening of the central core of insight. He also had enough confidence in the power of truth to believe that, if Christianity should come into competition with pagan cults, then it would be Christianity that should conquer and not paganism.

Of course, the expansionist policy had its perils. In various degrees, and at various times, it meant compromise, adjustment, assimilation of alien elements, and even a temporary diluting of the doctrine. For those who insist upon being utterly pure in act as well as pure in heart, this is the first step toward the corruption of the whole man. They do not believe that what springeth from within can cleanse again what is laid on from without. They are like those servants who would cut down the wheat, because the enemy had come and planted tares in its midst. But it is a poor brand of wheat that cannot withstand a few tares. And in this world there is no separating of the wheat and the tares till the coming of the Lord of the Harvest. As for those who are too fearful of the tares, they will not even plant their wheat, and the grain will rot in the seed-bins.

Furthermore, it is an error to speak of medieval monasticism as though it were an instance of surrender to the isolationist temper. It is important here to distinguish between the anchorites and the regular clergy. The anchorite was a spiritual isolationist who wished to do with his religion what Plato wished to do with his philosophy. He cut himself off from the affairs of this world, and was content if he could but secure his own salvation. The monastic orders, on the other hand, were militant missionary organizations which pioneered in reform, in social and economic rehabilitation, in education, and in religious discovery. They called to their standards men of energy, spirit, and adventure, as much as the quiet recluse. Benedict, Dominic, Bernard, Francis, Loyola— these men were hardly isolationists! If there was any retreat in their manœuverings, it was the strategic sort of retreat that enabled them to conquer in this world as well as to win the crown in the next.

The critic who finds in monasticism nothing but a withdrawal from life is as deluded as that type of modern historian who, not comprehending how some men could love risk more than security, can account for the great procession of pioneers in American history only by saying that these were neurotics who could not adjust themselves to the complexities of civilized life, and therefore escaped to the primitive conditions of the frontier. But, if the flight is from the City of Destruction, then it is only the neurotics who remain at home.

In any case, medieval monasticism was simply an expression of that missionary impulse which is the initial token of vitality and the subsequent cause of continued growth in any living religion. For the history of Christianity, seen in larger perspective, is the history of Christian missions. The domestic church, in whatever locality, might appear to be casting its bread gratuitously on the waters when it sent its emissaries to distant places; yet it did not fail to find it again. For if the work of evangelization did not at once bear fruit in heathen lands, nevertheless it brought forth in abundance at home. It was the missionary movement more than anything else which kept the local church from sinking into Pharisaic self-complacency, which maintained in clear and vivid outline the larger goal of human brotherhood under God, and which pierced the crust of customary piety with the upthrust of new problems to be dealt with and of new possibilities to be realized in the Christian faith.

Moreover, it is a sure sign of the decay of religion at home when the missionary impulse begins to fail. Indeed, it is both cause and symptom. It is a cause of decay, in that the domestic church separates itself from the wider Christian fellowship and adventure in which alone it can find real fulfillment. It is a symptom of decay, in that it reflects the loss of that spiritual *élan vital* which impels the disciples of any living religion to leap forth —like Archimedes—in the midst of their lustrations, and to run half-naked among the peoples of the earth, crying, "Eureka! I have found it!" It is interesting, also, to note how the apologetic of the religious isolationist parallels that of the political isolationist. In each case, there is much virtuous patter about not meddling in the affairs of others, and about minding one's own affairs at home. In neither case is it seen that one's own affairs are intricately entangled with the affairs of others. In both cases the net outcome of not meddling in the affairs of others is that one attends inadequately to his affairs at home.

However, this sort of isolationism has never been a predominant mood in the Christian tradition. On the contrary, it might be said that the peculiar glory of Christianity has been that it has never been content to mind its own business. Thus it is that we note in the history of Christianity—in contrast to the history of some other religions—an extraordinary talent for getting into trouble, and an equally extraordinary talent for extracting from that trouble some fresh insight into truth, some new device of spiritual discipline, that shall illuminate the mind and elevate the soul of man. To be specific, I believe it is accurate to say that no other great historic religion has been tested against such a diversity of social, political, and economic institutions; has had to compete so continuously with independent and secular systems of ethics and philosophy; and has had to bear up under such a direct frontal attack from science and from the technology of an industrialized society. Christianity has meddled with all of these things, and all of these things have meddled with Christianity. And those who follow the expansionist Paul rather than the isolationist apostles will continue to believe that, out of this meddling and intermingling, there develops a secular society more purified in its vision and a religious faith more strengthened in its ideals.

It is also worth asking just why Christianity has never succumbed to isolationism. Part of the answer can be found in the remark of Spinoza that "the good which each one who follows virtue desires for himself, he also desires for other men." The good, then, which is the love of God and of man as known through Christ—unlike the good which is found in the love of Mammon—is a good of which the values are enriched and enhanced through sharing and through communication. Again, there is, in the Christian tradition, a discipline in charity which forbids one to rest content in the enjoyment of a good when there are others who have it not; and a discipline in humility, which will not allow even the ninety and nine that are saved to believe that their souls are worth more in the sight of God than the soul of the one lost sheep that is not in the master's fold. But, most important, perhaps, are an indefeasible faith in the will of God as it operates through the perplexities of history, and a hard core of realism, sprung from the cross of Christ, which forestalls both a cheap belief in the easy achievement of the ideal and a cheap skepticism of the efficacy whatsoever of the ideal.

IV

If the preceding statement is correct, then pacifism, so far as it is a form of spiritual isolationism, is a departure from the main tradition of Christianity. Pacifism isolates the works of love from the works of justice—an isolation which is ironical insofar as justice is the true foundation of peace. *Justitiae opus pax!* But pacifism also isolates the value of peace from the other values of love; and one cannot help feeling that it is a peculiarly negative and static view of love which finds its principal expression in peace.

Before this matter is explored more fully, it is important to make clear just what is under consideration. It is a principle, not a personality, which stands under judgment. Human personalities are always more complex than human doctrines. One may value the fellowship of an individual pacifist on account of his intellectual brilliance, or on account of his qualities of charity, humility, sincerity, and devotion. One must remember, also, that war and peace are not the only issues that confront Chris-

tians, and that the man whose teaching is repudiated today for its pacifism may, on a future occasion and in other
circumstances, display a spiritual sensitivity and a moral
courage which are superior to those of others. Moreover,
the pacifist, if he is a good Christian, will grant as much
as this to his opponent. To make this concession is simply
to make acknowledgment of the practical value of the
democratic tradition of freedom of speech and freedom
of conscience. But a high regard for the person of the
individual pacifist and for his other potentialities should
never preclude a rigorous scrutiny of the pacifist doctrine
in its implications for general Christian strategy, and in
its bearing upon the immediate situation.

In conducting such an examination, one of the first
things to be noted is that, in many of our American denominations, too many churchmen are still on the de-
fensive psychologically with respect to pacifism. It may
be that, as members of the state, men readily ac-
knowledge their duty to fight, but, as members of the
church of Christ, they have a subconscious feeling that
he who does not fight in this war is somehow a better
man than the one who does fight. The liberal-minded
Christian patriot may be willing to say that this is as it
should be. But it takes a peculiar turn when a chaplain in
the armed forces is obliged almost to apologize for dar-
ing to appear in uniform at one of his denominational
assemblies; and when, on the college campus, the conscientious objector who goes to camp is promptly saluted
as a courageous Christian, while the ordinary fellow who

goes off to risk his life on the battlefield is greeted as a good patriot, but is viewed as one whose status as a Christian may be somewhat under suspicion. What we have here is a situation where a small minority, buttressed by the prestige of a twenty-year tradition of pacifism in the church, is actually able to exert a moral influence out of all proportion to its numbers, and sometimes beyond the bounds of the requirements of democratic and Christian liberties.

At the same time, there is raised the extraordinary question as to whether or not the church is really involved in the war. On strictly empirical grounds the answer is so obvious, as to make one wonder how such a query should have been introduced in the first place. Part of the confusion arises from the failure to distinguish between the church as an ecclesiastical organization, and the church as the larger fellowship of Christian men and women in society. Here, it seems to me, the observations of Rauschenbush are still pertinent. There are certain institutions which, in principle, have accepted the Christian ideal: these are the church, the family, the school, and the democratic state. Still somewhat beyond the pale is the economic order, and far beyond the pale is the field of international relations. To talk, then, of retiring to the catacombs is to recommend a strategy that was applicable only at a time when Christian principles had not been accepted by the family, by the schools, and by a democratic state. Such a strategy would be a betrayal of basic Christian institutions in favor of one institution, the church proper, which can be regarded now as only one focal point in the total Christian fellowship.

Obviously there are only three possible courses of action with reference to war. Two of these are isolationist procedures; and the third is the pluralistic blend of pragmatism. One may emphasize military proficiency, and try to isolate it from any corruption by Christian principles: this the Nazis propose to do, and are doing successfully. Or, forgetting justice, one may emphasize Christian love, and try to isolate it from all contamination by the brutalities of war: this the pacifists propose to do. Or one may mingle the motifs of justice, and love, and military valor, in a compound which is as shocking and incredible to the Nazi purist in war as it is to the Christian purist in peace, and trust that, out of this mixture, there may emerge, not the ideal victory of arms, nor the ideally just and durable peace, but an adequate victory in arms, and a more just and more enduring peace. In any case, if the principles enunciated in this essay are sound, both the Nazi and the pacifist isolationists will defeat themselves, and the field will be held by the impure pragmatists who are not afraid to temper their gold with the baser metal.

Actually, of course, the pacifist is no more able to isolate himself from all involvement in the brutalities of war than the Nazi militarist is able to cut himself off from all reckoning with a humanitarian conscience. The great traditions of pacifism within Christianity recognize this situation. It is part of the genius of an historic discipline in pacifism, like that of the Quakers, that it is realistically aware of the difficulties to be faced. So it is that the Quakers, while following a partially isolationist strategy, manage to avoid the purely negative implications of popular pacifism and show an extraordinary aptitude at being the first to be on hand when there is some constructive and sacrificial work of love to be done. Elton Trueblood, in an essay on "Vocational Christian Pacifism," * has made an admirable statement of the underlying doctrine. On strictly pragmatic grounds this position is unimpeachable. And it must be confessed that those who follow this program appear to be endowed with at least one of the great gifts of the Spirit.

Unfortunately, popular pacifism is never so open-eyed and so realistic as this. Too often, while claiming aloofness from the whole conflict, it serves indirectly as the tool of one of the contending interests. Certainly the popular pacifist in America, before Pearl Harbor, was carrying out the propaganda purposes of Adolf Hitler, through personal conviction, with more efficiency than if he had been a paid agent of the Nazi state. Moreover, his type of pacifism was usually the idealistic front for a selfish nationalism which ran counter to every kind of Christian principle. What a horrible medley of discordant notes came out of this symphony can be discerned by turning the pages of the back issues of any one of several popular religious periodicals in America, and remarking

* Cf. *Christianity and Crisis*, November 3, 1941.

the number of times that the bass sounds of provincial patriotism actually break through the sweet melody of high-toned idealism.

All that is tawdry enough; but the case of Kagawa's last visit to the United States has sinister implications. It must be inquired, with the most uncompromising severity, why it was that this distinguished pacifist and Christian leader, after having been thought dangerous enough to the Japanese war effort to be taken into protective custody by the state, should have been released by the Japanese Government at the time he was released, to make a visit to the United States to proclaim, among other things, his particular brand of the doctrine of non-resistance. Part of the burden of Kagawa's message in this country was a complaint of the bellicose attitude of Americans toward Japan. One remembers that this theme was taken up by the pacifistic flagellants of the religious press and made the occasion for much searching of heart and humble self-mortification. The conclusion is inescapable that the Japanese Government chose to utilize this idealist as a means, either for reinforcing in America the mood of non-intervention, or for further beclouding our vision before the coup at Pearl Harbor. Of course, these are insufficient grounds for condemning the man, Kagawa, whose sincerity of purpose cannot for one moment be doubted, and whose constructive achievements in other fields are more than enough to atone for this, or for any other mistake he may make. But it does illustrate, with nasty vividness, how too pure a pacifism may be used as a cover for designs that are diabolically Machiavellian.

Mahatma Gandhi makes another illuminating study. Gandhi is neither so naïve as Kagawa, nor so unqualified in his pacifism as a good Quaker. Actually, his absolute is national independence for India, while non-resistance is the means to this end. If peace were his primary objective, then he would acquiesce in British rule; for, if the British brought nothing else to India, they did bring it more peace than it had ever known before. Indeed, Gandhi is to be extolled for his statesmanship more than for his saintliness. In non-resistance he has a strategy for national independence that works—in India, and against Britain. It works in India, because it accords with the *mores* of the people—with the age-old Hindu tradition of non-injury to any living thing. It works against Britain, because British statesmen and soldiers—unlike those of Nazi Germany and of Japan—are occasionally disturbed by a Christian conscience, and because the achievement of dominion status by other British colonies gives warrant that, in time, India, too, may achieve autonomy. Yet it must be clear that the attainment of independence by India must eventuate, not in a great pacifist culture, but in one more powerful national state armed to the teeth like the others; just as it is clear that, when independence has been won, the simple village crafts espoused by the Mahatma will give way to vast industrial organizations. Within limits, certainly, Gandhi is the shrewdest kind of pragmatist in his strategy for the attainment of immediate ends; but he is also a shrewd enough opportunist not to let the purity of his present ideal be sullied by a consideration of the consequences that must inevitably follow when it is realized.

Verily, the pure in heart are the blessed. And how conveniently do they forget that other saying of Scripture, that they are to be judged by their fruits. John Dewey has pointed out that, in every act, there is the intended consequence, and there are the collateral consequences. It is a mark of maturity in morals to attempt to calculate the collateral consequences of an act, and to accept responsibility for them as well as for the intended consequence. But the purist, or the fanatic, pays regard only to the intended consequence. So it is that, though the collateral consequences of a course of action should overwhelm more sensitive men with a feeling of ignominious defeat, the starry-eyed idealist remains forever pure in heart through contemplation of that consequence alone which he intended, even though it should never have been brought to pass. This is the drawing power of absolutism over pragmatism for all delicate souls.

But, while the isolationism of the pacifist has too often been a spurious one, that has permitted him to become the unwitting instrument of unworthy interests, there are two instances in which the logic of his position seems to have been consummated. One instance is the C.O. camp. Here an initial spiritual isolation is fulfilled in physical and social isolation. Here, retiring from the "infection of lawlessness spreading over the rest of mankind," the pacifist must be content "if he can, in any way, live his life untainted in his own person by unrighteousness and unholy deeds." One may respect both the conscience and the courage of the individual who finds himself in such a spot, but one cannot help feeling that there is a certain poetic justice in his sentence.

The pacifist, moreover, has isolated himself from the peace-table. For it should not be thought, for one moment, that those who have not contributed directly toward the sacrifices for winning the war, or toward the agonies of the battlefield, shall be asked to come in, as visiting angels, to lay down the terms of the final settlement. So it is that the pacifist, because he will not participate in the taint of the war-maker, is cut off from the blessedness of the peace-maker.

Once again, isolationism defeats itself.


**v**


As a national policy, isolationism in the United States is dead for the moment. It came to a spectacular end in the catastrophe of Pearl Harbor. Moreover, there are hopeful indications that many Americans are firmly resolved that henceforth their country shall play its proper rôle in the world family of nations. Yet we should not delude ourselves into believing that, because we have forsaken the practice of isolationism, we have all at once lost the isolationist temper. Habits of thinking do not change so rapidly as the patterns of overt action. In any case, it is instructive to consider the ethical character and overtones of isolationism as an American phenomenon.

Part of its source lay in primitive national selfishness and provincial patriotism. Like all forms of selfishness, this sort of nationalism was so attentive to the needs of its narrower self, that it frustrated the possibilities of its larger self, and, finally, defeated the ends of its narrower self. How purblind it was to the meaning of events in the world in which it lived can be read in any of the pronouncements of a number of isolationist senators before America's entry into the war. And that it continues in an identically selfish stupidity can be read in the pronouncements and attitudes of the same senators after America's entry into the war. For these senators, who once would have nothing to do with any other country, are now the most greedy and vengeful in their attitude toward other nations. They seek to atone for their erstwhile passivity by ferocious outcries and savage gesticulations which are contrary, not only to the principles of an intelligently ordered peace, but even to the purposes of an efficiently designed military campaign.

At its very best, this kind of Americanism projects, on a national scale, the dilemma of the individual who cannot establish a continuity between his personal and his public morality. In the United States, such a man is, typically, a good husband, a loving father, a loyal church member, and a leader in community affairs, sacrificially giving time and money to local interests. At the same time, however, he is unscrupulous in his relations with his business competitors, ruthless in his attitude toward labor, and disregardful of his duty to the nation as a whole. Within a narrow circle of obligation, his morality is of the very highest, but, beyond this area, he reverts to the most primitive standards of conduct. Moreover, his range of vision and of ethical sensitivity is correspondingly limited, so that the conviction of his own rectitude in personal matters is never troubled by an awareness of his savagery in the larger relations of life.

Similarly, there are too many of our congressional leaders who have distinguished themselves as champions of internal reform, but who have shown themselves to be blind reactionaries in foreign policy. Borah, Johnson, and Wheeler may be listed as outstanding examples. Their heroic battle for progressive causes within the domestic scene is matched only by their obdurate obstructionism in the face of programs designed to raise the moral quality of our relations to other countries. And if, at times, the influence of such men has been great upon our people, it is just because they symbolize vividly, on the political level, that break between local loyalties and larger loyalties which is characteristic of the split personality of the American individualist.

In another phase, isolationism was an expression of that spiritual torpor that overcame the American people after suffering frustration in their first effort to fight a war to make the world safe for democracy. There then developed an amazing apologetic for inaction, which said that democracy and war are intrinsically incompatible, and that fighting for freedom is the best way to destroy freedom. How frequently these phrases were repeated, and how widely they were believed, was a measure, for the moment, of the utter degradation of the American spirit. For these assertions are about as completely contrary to fact as any that could be made. Indeed, there has been hardly any great democracy in the history of the world—Athens, Switzerland, France, Great Britain, the United States—which, as a rule, was not born in a revolutionary war, which has not survived a civil war, and which has not fought several foreign wars, and—provided it was victorious—come out of these conflicts stronger in its democratic liberties than it was before. As for the extermination of liberties through defeat, even Machiavelli knew what a rare occurrence is that, when he remarked that "he who becomes master of a city accustomed to freedom and does not destroy it may expect to be destroyed by it."

It was another expression of this spiritual torpor that the proposal should be made, that the United States stay out of the war, but that it step in at the end, with all its resources intact, to dictate the peace, to bind up the wounds of the nations, and to enforce a world order in accord with its own democratic principles. Thus Uncle Sam was to be metamorphosed into Lady Bountiful with a box of chocolates in one hand and a policeman's nightstick in the other. The lazy idealism which engendered this sweet dream could not understand that the beneficence of him who offers salvation without sharing in the agony of the cross begets resentment, not gratitude, hatred, not love.

But, in addition to disillusioned idealism and to primitive national selfishness, American isolationism was deeply rooted in the hedonistic humus of a bourgeois culture. This becomes strikingly evident if we translate the individual ethics of Epicureanism into a political ethics for the United States. Living during the decline of Roman civilization, the Epicurean developed a kind of monasticism which, unlike the monasticism of the Middle Ages, was literally a retreat from the world. What he wanted out of life was pleasure: so he refrained from business activity—except to draw on his private income; took no part in politics—unless to hold a sinecure; abstained from matrimony—unless he could find a rich wife; ignored logic and learning—except so far as it might free his mind from superstition; and avoided both religion and wrong-doing, because either one or the other might spoil his sleep and upset his digestion. So, with a few like-minded fellows, he retired to his garden, there to enjoy his pleasures undisturbed by the follies of the busy world of ambitious men.

The individual American, it is true, entered with zest into all the activities which the Epicurean disdained. But it is also true that what he sought was pleasure. He confined himself, moreover, to his own fellowship of choice spirits, and looked with dismay on the unruly strife of the wild beasts in foreign lands. His garden, where he held his retreat, was, of course, a bigger and better garden than any dreamed of by Epicurus. It took in all the broad acres of America, so "beautiful for spacious skies, for amber waves of grain, for purple mountain majesties above the fruited plain."

Safely ensconced within this hedonist's paradise, the American isolationist, if he had been a classical scholar, might have spent many a pleasant hour savoring the verses of the wise Lucretius. No doubt he would have been disturbed by the rather meagre material basis of the Epicurean's pleasures. But, in these years of world chaos and turmoil, there were a few lines of the poet that he could appreciate to the full: "It is sweet when the winds disturb the waters on the vast deep, to behold from the land the great distress of another—not because it is joyous pleasure that any one should be made to suffer, but because it is agreeable to see from what evils thou thyself art free. It is also sweet to contemplate the contending forces of war, arrayed over the plains, without any share of thine own in danger."

But, as the American Epicurean was also something of a Pharisee, it came to pass that, on Thanksgiving Day of 1941, he went up into the temple to pray, and spake thus with himself: "O Lord, I thank thee that my people are not as other peoples are—nor even as yon Nazi and yon Britisher—murderous in their evil devices, given to war and to carnage. I thank thee that, though the sons of other nations lie bleeding in their hospital beds, or lie slain on the battlefield, yet my sons are still sound of limb. I thank thee that, though the daughters of other nations may mourn for the lover or the son who returns not, or may lay down their bruised bodies in the ruins of bombed and burning villages, yet my daughters are still immaculate. O Lord, I thank thee, that thou hast favored my nation above all other nations of the earth!"

Was it Tertullian, or another one of the church fathers, who taught that a chief delight of the saints in heaven was the privilege of looking down upon the tortures of the damned in hell, and of observing at length the terrible agonies of less fortunate souls? A tenderhearted modernism, proud of its ethical sensitivity, was quick to repudiate the cruel immorality of such a picture. Yet this ethical sensitivity was, for the most part, silent before the spectacle of a whole nation contemplating, with selfish sadism, the horrible torments of a world of suffering fellow-men.

Were we not a young people, it might be said that, at the moment, the United States had arrived at the condition of Rome in the period of its decline. The Goths and Vandals might threaten from afar. But the proud citizens of the empire would not soil their hands with blood. After all, they had their hired mercenaries to hold off the invader. They themselves must remain in Rome and preserve the civilized values! Besides, the barbarians were so far away. How could they ever hope to traverse the rivers, and forests, and mountains, that lay between them and Rome? No, Rome, the Eternal City, could never perish! "Surely the Lord is with us; no evil can befall *us*!"

But no destruction is too distant for a people that has betrayed its spiritual heritage! No ruin too remote for a nation sunk in the slough of pleasure, prosperity, and comfort!

## VI

It is also written, that men do not light a candle, and put it under a bushel, but on a candlestick; and it giveth light unto all that are in the house.

Whether we use the analogy of the candle, or of the talent, it is all one. The candle and the talent are the values of life—justice, love, righteousness, liberty, intelligence, beauty.

It is a false modesty that should hide the candle under a bushel, and it is a false economy that should hide the talent in the field. The candle under the bushel gives light to no one, and its light is the same as darkness. The talent in the field yields profit to no one, and its lustre is consumed by the rust.

Only when the talent moves freely in the marts of men can we prove its value. It matters not that it should be soiled a bit in circulation.

Only when the candle casts its light into the darkness can we know its true brilliance. And, if the light be filled with smoke, then we can trim the wick. But, when the light is clear, men may behold its good work, and glorify their Father which is in heaven.

*Three:*
# THE GADARENE
# DEMONIAC AND
# THE SWINE

*And they came over unto the other side of the sea, into the country of the Gadarenes.*

*And when he was come out of the ship, immediately there met him out of the tombs a man with an unclean spirit, who had his dwelling among the tombs; and no man could bind him, no, not with chains: Because that he had been often bound with fetters and chains, and the chains had been plucked asunder by him, and the fetters broken in pieces: neither could any man tame him. And always, night and day, he was in the mountains, and in the tombs, crying, and cutting himself with stones.*

*But when he saw Jesus afar off, he ran and worshipped him, And cried with a loud voice, and said, What have I to do with thee, Jesus thou Son of the most high God? I adjure thee by God, that thou torment me not. For he said unto him, Come out of the man, thou unclean spirit. And he asked him, What is thy name? And he answered, saying, My name is Legion: for we are many. And he besought him much that he would not send them away out of the country.*

*Now there was there nigh unto the mountains a great herd of swine feeding. And all the devils besought him, saying,*

*Send us into the swine, that we may enter into them. And forth-*
*with Jesus gave them leave. And the unclean spirits went out,*
*and entered into the swine: and the herd ran violently down a*
*steep place into the sea, (they were about two thousand,) and*
*were choked in the sea.*

*Mark 5:1–13.*

# 3:

# THE GADARENE
# DEMONIAC AND
# THE SWINE

ONE of the many disservices which the
feminist movement rendered to womankind was to degrade its status in theology. In the old days, when theology was an exclusively masculine enterprise, woman was
vividly portrayed as the historical root of original sin,
the cause of the fall of Adam, and the source of all the
calamities that have preyed upon the human race
throughout the ages. But with the coming of women's
rights, all this was changed. Now it was shown that Eve
was no more to be blamed than Adam, and that, even in
sinfulness, woman was no more exciting a creature than
mediocre man. This was one of the rewards of "emancipation."

But, however much this change of doctrine may appeal to the sense of equity, it rests on false psychological
assumptions. For, when woman was deprived of pre-
eminence in sinfulness, she was robbed of one of the most
distinguished achievements of a spiritual being. As usual,
the feminists in theology had misunderstood their own
sex as well as the rest of human kind. Indeed, most

71

women never resented their position in the older theology. They always felt more kinship with the Wife of Bath than with Patient Griselda, and were more secure in the heritage that came to them from their mother Eve than they were confident of the goal set up for them by the holy mother Mary. To know that, incarnate in one's own person—however unattractive it might be physically—lay the ancient source of the fall of man, and a dire menace to masculine peace of mind for all ages to come: now there was something to lend a fillip to the figure and a lilt to the step as one walked along the drab ways of this dull world!

What feminism did to women, modernism did for the whole race. It destroyed the glamour of sin. In the middle ages, there were seven very specific sins, and they were all known as deadly. Moreover, they were arranged in a hierarchy which showed a superb feeling for dramatic as well as for spiritual values; and the torments appropriate to each were vividly illustrated in the several orthodox handbooks to hell. Pride was the most awful of human trespasses. And what a thrill it must have been to the ordinary carnal creature to learn, from the words of the preacher, that he had in himself at least the potentiality of that Satanic sin, even though most of his pilgrimage on earth revealed only the more sordid vices of avarice, gluttony, and lust. So long as man knew that he could sin fearfully, he had a firmer faith in the high meaning of his destiny than could ever have been given him by the assurance of his calling to a life of saintliness.

Today we are rather hard put to it to satisfy our craving for sin, and for great sinners. Not only have the vices been made mediocre by enlightenment, but even Satan himself has been abolished. In the United States, the best we can do is to concentrate our attention on a few tame secular devils. For a certain number of people, Franklin D. Roosevelt is the Great Devil of today, as, for others, John D. Rockefeller was the Great Devil of a previous generation. On the works of darkness of either one might be blamed all business losses, the baby's colic, spiritual wickedness in high places, the decay of private morals, and one's betting losses at the race track. The fact that one of these men was the representative of a plutocratic order, and that the other is the representative of a social democracy is, from the point of view of high religion, quite irrelevant. The value of both lies in the reassurance they offer that, if mankind cannot scale the heights to holiness, at least it can still be splendidly wicked.

However, fascism has vastly outdone the dull democracies in satisfying the human need for Satanism. In this respect, Adolf Hitler is a spiritual portent of the first order—one that we could not at once recognize, because he stands far beyond the puny dimensions of our bourgeois demons. Yet here is one, magnificent like Lucifer, who roves, full of rage, like a roaring lion, to tempt, to betray, to destroy the souls of men, and to rob God of his glory. "And no man could bind him, no, not with chains: Because that he had been often bound with fetters and chains, and the chains had been plucked asunder by him, and the fetters broken in pieces: neither could any man tame him." A demon that will be neither appeased, nor confined; that must either destroy, or be destroyed: this is something to restore our faith in the human race!

The fact is, that the capacity to sin greatly is one of the marks of the spiritual vitality of a culture. Reinhold Niebuhr has made it clear that the possession of mind and of soul is no guarantee of rectitude in conduct. It is the sign, only, of maturity rather than infancy. In one sense, the important difference between a child and an adult is that the latter has developed his intellectual and spiritual powers. But it is also true that, with these matured abilities, the adult has greater potentialities for evil as well as for good. Herein lies the ambiguity of all progress. But, for childhood, there is only innocence; and, in an infantile civilization, there is neither great good nor great evil.

This enables us to see the pathos of the neo-orthodox theologian today who would have us recover our "sense of sin." He would do much better if he should encourage us to recover, first of all, our sins. How, indeed, can we be afflicted with the sense of an experience that we have not! Genuine sin is the privilege of a spiritual being. But we have not been spiritual beings. We have been vegetables—sunning ourselves contentedly as we felt about our roots the warmth of the well-rotted manure of our so much vaunted peace and prosperity.

A bit differently it might be said that we have had our sins, but we have been unwilling to be confronted with them. We have been ashamed to face them, not because the evil of them might char our souls, but because they have been cheap and ignominious beyond belief. We have paid tithe of mint, anise, and cummin, not only to God, but even to Satan. To contemplate a mediocre achievement in virtue, that can be borne by any mortal man; but to be negligent in vice, that were a disloyalty to one's heritage of natural depravity that could be tolerated by no human creature. How deep is this feeling in the breast of man can be noted by reviewing the ludicrous list of peccadilloes so eagerly confessed, in swank revival meetings, by those who are anxious to prove that, because there is in them something eminently worth damning, there must be in them also something eminently worth saving.

The literature of the Bible, when it is being realistic about human nature, rather than flattering, appears to be cognizant of this situation. Much of the time, people are compared to sheep and to cattle, rather than to devils. For the gentle ironist who was the author of the book of *Jonah*, it was the supreme measure of generosity in the love of God, that He should embrace with His fatherly care even such creatures as were found in the city of Nineveh—"sixscore thousand persons that cannot discern between their right hand and their left hand; and also much cattle." Yea, even for cattle hath the only begotten Son of God died on the cross! Perhaps this makes of Christianity, not a slave-morality, but, rather, a cattle-ethic.

If the authors of the Bible had been more sound in their theology, they would have compared the human race more frequently to swine. This would have proclaimed unequivocally the natural depravity of man. Or the unclean beast might have been used merely as a symbol of that contented animality into which man so easily falls. The sow that was washed returns to her wallowing. Likewise, the soul of man, even when it is washed in the blood of Christ, returns again to a complacent wallowing in the puddle of physical comforts and sensuous satisfactions.

The tale of the Gadarene demoniac may be said to figure forth, in dramatic fashion, both this pole and the other pole of human sinfulness. The demoniac may be taken as a symbol of pride—a fearful pride that cries out against God, that cuts itself and cuts others in its tormented and rebellious writhings, a pride that cannot be bound by human fetters, and that can be tamed by no man. The swine may be taken as a symbol of that spiritual uncleanness which is complacency in carnal delights. Under a social interpretation, the demoniac is a type of the destructive fury of a fascist culture. The swine are a type of the dull degradation of a bourgeois capitalism. For, in our day, in our country, there are no longer any demoniacs. One finds them only in the wild Gergesene coasts of Germany and of Japan. With us, for a long time now, there have been—only the swine!

## II

Complacency, as a central culture trait, has its own complex of attendant values and mechanisms. It has its own religion, its political methods, its program of education, and its ethics. Here, too, the vast resources of the human mind and spirit are called into play to produce an intricately patterned civilization—even though it be only a civilization of pigs.

In the rationale of complacency, one holds to the peak of human virtue by being good-natured at all costs. No solicitations of the ideal, no challenges to moral endeavor, no ecstasies of art may be permitted to disturb that tranquillity of mind which is so needful for tranquillity of the stomach. The "Good Joe" and the "Good Sport" are the true heroes of this culture: not the good sport who bears up under physical discomfort because it cannot touch his soul, but the good sport who is disregardful of spiritual affliction because it cannot touch his belly. The "Good Joe," indeed, suffereth long, and is kind; yet, actually, he suffereth not, because he feeleth not, and he is kind because he cares not. The "Good Joe," moreover, beareth all things, believeth all things, hopeth all things; for not to bear all things means to exert effort to change some things, and not to believe and to hope all things calls for too cruel a scrutiny of those values which are more comfortably taken for granted.

It should not be thought, however, that complacency

is without its own deep spiritual tensions, its agonies of the uncertain soul rent terribly on the horns of on the one hand and of on the other hand. Was not Buridan's ass, indeed, a tragic figure—standing midway betwixt a bale of hay and a pail of water—unable to determine whether its most pressing need were hunger or thirst—and perishing thereby? But we do not, on that account, affirm the ass to be a martyr or a saint. For a saint must be torn between things other than mere hay and water. Water and hay—prosperity in our time, and peace in our time—hay and water: these were the two poles of our deepest spiritual tension!

But, apart from this, the complacent man is free from the torment of all lofty aspiration. He has proved, to his own satisfaction, that all ideals are "ideologies"—nothing but the rationalization of appetites and impulses as primitive as his own. It is true that when his own appetites are frustrated, he can, of a sudden, assume all the ferocity of an enraged boar in assaulting his enemies. But, for the rest, he carefully maintains that good-natured peacefulness of demeanor which alone is compatible with the peace of the belly. Thus, any debate about truth, goodness, and beauty, is dismissed as mere "propaganda." To allow oneself to be caught in dispute about these things is the final proof of imbecility, and to go to war over such dubious realities as justice, brotherhood, and liberty, is simply evidence of glandular over-activity linked with a stoppage of the passages in the intestinal tract. With respect to all such matters, the complacent man is dogmatically atheistic or scientifically agnostic. But any exhortation to build bigger and better barns and to store them with more grain is hailed—not as "propaganda"—but as an intelligent "educational program" and as a sound manifestation of "practical Christianity."

It is proved, also, that the only way to achieve the public good is to pursue one's private interest. The world of men is organized like the universe of Leibnitz: each person in it, a windowless monad, oblivious of all the living galaxy about him, serenely unfolds his own course, while, thanks to a pre-established harmony, his innocent egotism is transmuted into effective altruism. As Mandeville rather cynically expressed it:

> Thus every Part was full of Vice,
> Yet the whole Mass a Paradise.

Herbert Spencer, with the added weight of evolutionary doctrine, undertook to demonstrate that, on the one hand, altruism depends on egotism, and, on the other hand, egotism depends on altruism, and that, when we have finally developed the perfect industrial society, there will be a balance of these two motives in painless and effortless well-doing. And so, the wealth of the nation is made up of the profits of the individual, and only the individual who is relentless in private profiteering is a good citizen of the nation.

What should amaze the historian of morals is the way this doctrine has existed in our culture side by side with a Christian teaching that is explicitly opposed to it, without there being any marked awareness of the conflict in principle. For surely the dominant ethical tradition in Christianity has always taught that the desires of the individual frequently go counter to the needs of society, and that any society which is to be distinguished by spiritual achievement must have in it many persons who are willing to sacrifice their personal interests for the sake of the public welfare. Even in the demonic culture of fascism, this much is known. And as John Dewey has pointed out, a genuinely evolutionary theory, not perverted by a mechanistic rationalism, would never suggest that a time will come when the performance of duty will be painless. But the complacent man does not believe in pain, or duty, or sacrifice; he cares only for comfort.

Another device in the technique of complacency is to adopt the attitude of a false humility. This has at least two modes. One mode is that of repentance of a lesser failing in order to divert attention from a more fundamental defect. Thus the American isolationist—now that we are in the war—may beat his breast dramatically over our failure to build great armaments in time of peace, and yet say nothing about what we have done to contribute to the causes of the war, or about what we might have done to forestall the original outbreak of the war in Europe. The other mode is that of affecting a humility which pretends to be unworthy to pass judgment on debated issues, for fear that, should one be drawn into the debate, it might disturb his comfort. At the beginning of this conflict, for instance, there were many Americans who, on domestic issues, would express their opinions unhesitatingly and with the utmost violence; and yet, when asked to decide between the Englishman and the German, between democracy and fascism on the foreign scene, they were suddenly overcome by an access of Christian humility and of servile drooling about "After all, who am *I* to decide between the right of this and the wrong of that?"

Along with the religious virtue of humility, there is exploited a basic intellectual technique of science. This is to inquire into the "causes" of things. And yet, in this instance, never to consider the possible consequences of things. And so one examines learnedly the "causes" of the rise of the Nazi movement—curiously enough never going farther back in history than the date of the Ver-sailles Treaty; and the "causes" of imperialism, and the "causes" of wars, and the "causes" of Japanese expansion, and the "causes" of Hitlerism—everything, indeed, except the causes of one's own complacency. But, *tout savoir, c'est tout pardonner!*—is it not so? And completely to understand the "causes" of the mad dog that runs amuck in the community, that also is to forgive the mad dog, and to love him!

Verily, these are they of the understanding heart. And how to keep oneself free from all heroic commitment, and safe from all perilous adventure of the spirit—that they understand best of all!—Indeed, is it not written,

Judge not, lest ye be judged? And who are we to judge any one—least of all ourselves? Who knows?—perhaps if we let go the mote in our neighbor's eye, he will still be blind to the beam in our own eye!

But Mencius had a name for these fellows; he called them the "thieves of virtue." Job had a name for them; he called them "God's sycophants." Such are the "good, careful men of the villages!"

III

Education for complacency is one of the finely developed arts of a bourgeois civilization. While the two democracies of Great Britain and the United States have been equally devoted to this value, it must be said that, when it comes to integrating complacency with the school program, the younger country has outstripped its parent culture. There is, in the British people, a regrettable backwardness, a sentimental attachment to ancient traditions, which keeps them from putting into effect the thorough-going revisions which are necessary for social and intellectual advance. So it is that the American people, with their bolder, experimental attitude toward life, have been able to make more noteworthy progress in the enshrinement of complacency in education.

The key to the program is a simple one. One of the chief enemies of complacency is thought. Creative thinking may be said to be a blend of observation, insight, passion, and logical discipline. In the education for complacency, then, the child in school will be encouraged to see, to feel, to react, to bump into problems, and to initiate projects, but never to undergo that logical discipline which is needed to convert primitive, impulsive activity into rational activity. *L'homme qui médite est un animal dépravé.* Our children are to be animals undepraved!

In the study of history, this has meant a break-down of the sense of chronology, of long range patterns of causality, and the loss of any feeling for a common cultural heritage in civilization. History appears as a kind of glorified grab-bag, from which one selects characters, or events, according to taste and inclination, without being subject to the constraint of any objective order. And the historian, as pedagogue, becomes like a garrulously clucking hen, which, with outstretched wings, conducts its brood about the barnyard—pecking eagerly at stray seeds and roots of sustenance, and, happily, pulling up a live earth worm: whereat the whole flock comes bustling excitedly to the newly found treasure, each one trying to get its beak into the business, and withal making a great commotion together.

In the study of English language and literature, the tendency is to eliminate grammar. No more parts of speech, no more mechanical parsing, no more stupid diagramming of sentences; no more vain inquiry into the respective functions of commas, semicolons, and colons; no more topic sentences for paragraphs, no more "unity, coherence, and emphasis" for essays; no more even of the alphabet! As one principal of a "progressive" school informed me, the order of the alphabet is a matter of pure convention, anyway, and its only conceivable value is for the filing clerk. Apparently, then, one is not concerned either with dictionaries or with encyclopaedias! The general assumption is that, if the child can be taught, by conditioned reflex, to speak the language correctly without benefit of grammar, then he is much better off doing well what he ought to do if he doesn't know what he is doing.

The distaste for grammar carries over, in a peculiar way, into a distaste for the study of foreign languages. —And, be it said parenthetically, that all foreign languages are dead languages to the culture of complacency, which does not wish to have the peace of its own provincialism disturbed by alien elements.—In any case, the child who is ignorant of the grammar of his own language faces a double burden in mastering the grammar of another language. This places on the foreign language teacher the unpleasant onus of carrying out, in his department, a drill and a discipline which should have been well initiated in another department. It then becomes easy to prove that the study of foreign languages is a mechanical and routine affair, without genuine cultural value, and to suggest that probably this study, in the colleges, ought to be dropped in favor of more courses in education. The vicious circle is complete when the student, whose ignorance of the grammar of his native tongue makes it impossible for him to master the grammar of a foreign tongue, quits the study of the foreign tongue, and so ends up twice confirmed in ineptitude in the grammar of his own language.

The decline of mathematical studies has been part of the same trend. Here was one of the purest intellectual disciplines, which, far from having any obvious values in the immediate socialization of the individual, seemed to require, in its more advanced stages, an almost monastic calm and isolation of the mind. At the beginning, moreover, it called for training, by mechanical rote, in habits of counting, addition, subtraction, division, and multiplication, which, it was feared, might impair the beautiful spontaneity and freshness of the child's intelligence. Consequently, the elements of arithmetic were to be shuffled through over a despairing length of time, in such a manner as to leave the youngster, upon graduation from high school, with enough wisdom to calculate the accounts of his *Saturday Evening Post* route, but with a wholesome feeling that, if he should go on to college, mathematics, like philosophy or theology, was only for the abnormal and more introverted mind.

No one knows better than this writer that such an outcome is contrary to the whole spirit and method of Dewey's teaching. His book on *Democracy and Education* is still the classic statement of a constructive procedure for the schools of America. Moreover, far from repudiating logical disciplines, Dewey has written most extensively on the subject of logic, and has wished simply to substitute for the old, formal logic an experimental

logic that should be still more rigorous in its requirements of intellectual integrity and precision. For over
fifty years, he has been our most vigorous critic of the
kind of sensationalism which stops at the level of mere
feeling and impulse and biological activity, and fails
to go on to that matured activity which is truly intelligent.

However, in one of his more recent books—*Experience and Education* (1939)—Dewey seems to be aware
that something has gone wrong, although he is not quite
clear as to why things have gone wrong. What has happened is that the whole force of the *mores* of complacency has gone counter to his intention. His criticism of
formal logic has been made a pretext for the abolition of
all logic. His appreciation of the value of spontaneity in
a growing activity has been perverted into an emphasis
upon impulsiveness in activities that do not grow. His
method of free and open discussion has been used by
clever pedagogues as a more subtle device for indoc-
trination. His emphasis upon consultation of all interests
and the sharing of responsibility through committees has
been exploited by unscrupulous administrators to put up
the pretense of democracy while still retaining powers
that are autocratic. The plaudits that go to originality in
educational procedures have been employed to gain a
cheap notoriety in professional circles, while they also
served as a cover for a failure to do the job in funda-
mentals. And too often these pseudo-progressives in
education have been able to go on from one triumph to

another simply by using as the criteria of value, in their elaborate statistical reports on new experiments, their own bottomless standards of social and intellectual illiteracy.

The student—if we may call him such—who is the product of this program is an amazing specimen of educated ineptitude. He has been forbidden to perform tasks of rote memorizing in school, with the result that his memory is only loaded the more abundantly with all the trivia of ephemeral interests and current fads. He knows nothing of either the order or the scope of history, with the consequence that he stands unrooted like a tumbleweed blown over the prairies of life by every wind of doctrine. He is untrained in mathematics, when the whole trend of a technological culture calls for just that particular discipline. He is ignorant of foreign languages at the very moment when his nation is about to assume a still more significant rôle in its relationship to other countries. His lack of schooling in grammar is reflected both in an amazing incompetence in the English language, and in an inability to follow the most rudimentary rules of logic. His adjustment to his world is a static one, not a dynamic one, and the socialization which has been so carefully cultivated in him turns out to be nothing more than a socialization in the prevailing culture of complacency. It is little wonder, then, that, looking upon such a product, one sees, not so much the leader of a new progressivism for our world, but a mind that has been ruined almost beyond redemption.

IV

The clue to the politics of complacency is the same as the clue to education for complacency. The essential matter is to eliminate occasions for the exercise of mind or of soul—of thought, or of aspiration. Political activity is deprived of soul by the assumption that its concerns are of a narrowly routine and practical order, and it is stripped of mind by the assumption that its problems are primarily technical and administrative rather than problems of policy.

It was easy to do this in the orthodox capitalist state, where the function of government was conceived to be simply that of a passive policeman. Men of energy, intellect, and idealism were drained off into the pursuits of business and of technology, while politics was allowed to attract to its ranks the less imaginative functionaries. This has never been true of Great Britain to the extent that it has been true of the United States, because Great Britain has been an empire where politicians must at least pretend to be statesmen, while the United States has been a province almost self-contained within its own boundaries. Just how well this program has been realized in the United States, however, may be seen by noting the long list of rather ordinary persons who have occupied the American presidency in the interval from Lincoln to Wilson. During that interval it was enough to be just a little above the ordinary—like Taft, or Theodore

Roosevelt—to be greeted as a leader of outstanding ability.

In any case, the politics of complacency proceeds on the assumption that there are no real issues to be discussed by the public. While this mood prevails, it is almost impossible to tell the difference between the Republican and the Democratic parties. It can be said only that one party is in, and that the other party is out; that one party is gorging itself gloriously at the gravy-bowl, while the other scrambles under the table for a few forgotten crumbs. At election time, of course, it is needful to have several trumped-up issues, which can be discussed with fury to give the voting public the illusion of participating in significant debate. The successful politicians, under these circumstances, are those who display the greatest cunning and ingenuity in inventing spectacular but trivial issues to catch the public attention, while the basic values of the culture of complacency remain unchallenged. Unfortunately, at this time of genuine national peril, there survive too many of these politicians whose talent for exploiting spurious issues has finally made them unable to understand the real crisis.

The fine gradations of accomplishment in the arts of complacency exhibited by our national leaders are worth considering. Here, at the risk of some pedantry, I propose to apply John Dewey's analysis of the five steps in thinking, or problem-solving. The first step is to be aware of the existence of a problem. The second step is to analyze the problem for its significant features. The third step is to think up hypotheses, or courses of action, which may be fruitful in the solution of the problem. The fourth step is a systematic study of the implications of each proposed course of action; a comparison of the respective merits of these hypotheses; and the selection of the most likely one for action. The fifth step is the action itself.

When the career of Franklin D. Roosevelt is examined in the light of this logical framework, his peculiar talents are at once evident. As a man of action—not a man of complacency—he excels in steps one, three, and five. First of all, he has an extraordinary awareness of the existence of problems. His political opponents feel that he is aware of too many, and complain of the series of "crises" which have attended his years in office. In the case of the imminence, and then of the implications of the Second World War, however, Mr. Roosevelt's sensitivity certainly served his nation well. His next talent is for thinking up hypotheses, or programs of action, for dealing with his problems. Undoubtedly the New Deal has been marked by an amazing proliferation of such hypotheses—or "theories," as the Republicans prefer to call them. The final talent is for vigorous, bold, and incisive action—carried out with that delicate sense of timing which marks the master politician. One may criticize Mr. Roosevelt for his inadequacies in steps two and four: for failure to analyze his problems sufficiently; for failure to scrutinize carefully, in advance, the possible consequences of his various pet hypotheses. It is at these points that the intelligent critic of the administration—like Wendell Willkie—finds the flaws. But, as a logician might say, Mr. Roosevelt has been operating under temporal pressure: he has rarely had time for the careful work of analysis and of deduction that is called for in the ideal solution of a problem. Indeed, it is evidence of his great genius as a statesman, that his intuitive awareness of problems, his quick sense for what should be done, and his bold manner of doing it have, in spite of the lack of leisurely analysis, brought so much good to his country.

Herbert Hoover illustrates another emphasis in this logical pattern. He has always been honest enough to recognize a problem, if he could see it. His special genius, however, is found in step two, the analysis of the problem. It is only when he has plenty of time—as in suggesting the outlines for a new order after the peace—that he does fairly well in step three, the proposal of courses of action. His one term as president, however, has its chief value for logic as a study in the political possibilities of step two. For it would seem that Mr. Hoover spent most of his time in the thorough-going analysis of problems—prohibition, law-breaking, the depression—but that he hardly ever got around to significant action. This is the characteristic failing of the intelligent conservative. Indeed, the more intelligent and the more careful Mr. Hoover was in his analyses, the more certain it was that nothing important would ever be done. Furthermore, in the effort to understand, first the depression, and then the war, his categories of analysis were so outmoded—(Mr. Hoover is our best living representative, in the twentieth century, of the eighteenth-century mind)—that he failed utterly to get hold of the really significant features of the problem. He illustrates, none the less, the farthest march of progress in logical inquiry that may be allowed within the framework of the politics of complacency.

But, naturally, it was Calvin Coolidge who gave us the supreme embodiment of this mood. He never got to step one. He never acknowledged the existence of a problem. This made thinking of any sort quite unnecessary. To borrow the colloquial language of baseball, he was a batter who never even got to first base, while the enthusiastic fans applauded his economy of energy, because they knew the game could not be lost anyway. Indeed, it was the great genius of Calvin Coolidge, as the spiritual leader of the culture of complacency, that he gave his followers a sense of utter security by the simple expedient of acting as though there were no problems to worry about. Herbert Hoover, a man of more intellectual integrity, was the unfortunate individual who had to come later and cope with some of the issues of which his predecessor was so blandly unaware. But that the spell of the peace of Coolidge—a peace that passed not the understanding because it was below the level of all understanding—is yet strong in its hold on the minds of men is shown by the many persons who still yearn, in infantile regression, for the return, to politics, of the sanctimonious do-nothingism of that high priest of a complacent prosperity.

V

It is an old observation that religion can be made to serve as an opiate. Hobbes said that the doctrines of religion should be believed, but not critically examined; that they were like pills for the sick—good to swallow, but bitter if chewed. Schopenhauer ironically recommended religion, along with card-playing, as one of the best palliatives for the miseries of life. The French traditionalist, de Bonald, himself a devout Catholic, compared religion to a lubricating oil—"like those oily substances which, in complicated machines, make for force without effort, and movement without noise, and lessen resistance and soften friction." Consequently, religion has not failed of a rôle in the culture of complacency.

Under the influence of the Marxist tradition, however, we have neglected to note that religion may be an opiate for the powerful and the prosperous, as well as for the poor. Indeed, it can be easily shown, by an appeal to history, that religion has just as often made pleasant the descent into destruction for a corrupt ruling class, as it has made congenial to the oppressed and the underprivileged their inferior position. In both cases, its functions are the same: to dull any sensitive awareness of real social evils; to offer cheap but exciting salvation from superficial ills; to blind the class in question to its organic relationship to other classes in society; and to endow the most critical disabilities of that class with an other-worldly meaning, which makes its gravest moral defects appear to be the tokens of high spiritual achievement.

In the culture of complacency, the chief function of any acceptable faith was to induce in its devotees a profound spiritual slumber. "Respect and modesty in the presence of sleep! That is the first thing! And to go out of the way of all who sleep badly and keep awake at night! . . . No small art is it to sleep: it is necessary for that purpose to keep awake all day! . . ." *Thus Spake Zarathustra!*—and Nietzsche was, for the nineteenth century, along with Carlyle, one of the great castigators of complacency—as Reinhold Niebuhr has been for our time. For sleep it is a wondrous thing, beloved from pole to pole—and those spiritual somnambulists who walk under its spell often display an amazing surefootedness on the thin edge of peril which should be impossible for any person in full possession of his faculties. For them, the only real danger is to be awakened. Alas, that we should ever have been awakened! For, now, not poppy, nor mandragora, nor all the drowsy syrups of the East shall ever summon us back to that sweet complacency which we once knew.

In the first centuries of the Christian era, it was Neo-Platonism which served as the religious opiate of the dying pagan world. It is important to note that the followers of Plotinus were the wealthy and aristocratic pagans, and that they included an emperor in their number. To them, Plotinus recommended apathy towards things of sense: this is easy for the rich, who have everything. To them, he spoke of matter as something base, a principle of evil which, nevertheless, if made into beautiful forms, might minister to spiritual insight: it took the rich to turn base matter into these beautiful forms; so they built luxurious homes for themselves—for spiritual purposes. Social ethics was of an inferior order. One should do his conventional duties as a citizen; but there was no sense in trying to reform, or to uplift, one's fellowman, or in trying to ameliorate his lot by philanthropy. That was too crass, and too materialistic! The only proper use of money was in the cultivation of beauty—the spiritual beauty of a magnificent estate. As for less fortunate folk—well, it was taught that the world was governed by a great harmony, and, in a perfect harmony, there must be a few discords. Plotinus' patrons were not among the discords. So they put their minds on higher things, and cultivated a sense for spiritual realities, while the rotten society of which they were the most rotten part gradually tumbled into ruin.

The counterpart of this luxurious, decadent mysticism has appeared, in the twentieth century, in a grosser bourgeois variant, within the very bosom of Christianity. Once more it attracts the wealthy and the aristocrats of a declining order, and sucks into its orbit the less privileged persons who wish to be spiritually identified with its more distinguished clientele. Its prestige as a religious movement derives, not from its following of publicans and sinners, but from its appropriating the honorable name of an ancient university for its title, from the acknowledgment of its leader that God, too, is a millionaire, from its sedulous cultivation of the best people, and from its care to hold its meetings in the best homes and in the best hotels. While its membership boasts no emperors, it does honestly aspire to include a few dictators, and, meanwhile, for lack of these, must be content with high officers of state, Yale football captains, presidents of chambers of commerce, and a smattering of congressmen and of members of parliament. In this mysticism, the truly devout are blessed with hunches, or with intuitions of spiritual insight, which enable them to proclaim the sovereign remedy, of the moment, for the problems of sex, or of economic depression, or of war, or of peace. But there is never anything so crassly materialistic as a reforming humanitarianism, and great care is taken to change only the hearts of men, but never to alter the conditions of the corrupt society in which they live. To those who can read the signs of the times, this religious movement is the last, self-deluding clutch after complacency of a spiritually rotten culture before it falls into utter destruction.

It is, however, a familiar tale with contemporary theologians, the way Christianity was pervaded with the spirit of complacency in recent decades. In theology, it meant an emphasis on God's love, with a disregard for

His power and His justice. In anthropology, it meant a rejection of the doctrine of original sin, in favor of a more optimistic view of man. In social ethics, it meant a naïve faith in the possibility of the early realization of the Kingdom of God on earth. In the practice of public worship, it included, among other things, a tendency to eliminate such grand old hymns as "Stand up, stand up for Jesus!" and "Onward Christian soldiers!" as being too full of militaristic connotations for the followers of the Prince of Peaceful Complacency. The corresponding development in the use of the Bible was a growing feeling that a truly civilized world could no longer tolerate the rough realism of the Old Testament, while, in the New Testament, all of the sayings of Jesus that dealt with persons being cast into "outer darkness, where there shall be weeping and wailing and gnashing of teeth" were carefully bleached from the record, and nothing was left of his teaching except sweetness and light and loveliness.

At some future time, indeed, the historian of religious sociology will find the height of irony in the recent modern handling of the doctrine of love in Christianity. For God's love is great and strong and tender; but it was converted into a slow ooze of indiscriminate benevolence which slopped over the sinner as it smeared the saint. Christ's love was governed by a spiritual insight which cherished men for what they might be rather than for what they were, and which was as stern in judgment as it was strong in forgiveness; but it was translated into a slimy sentiment which flattered trivial sins with the privilege of pardon, and exalted trifling virtues to the rank of high moral achievement. The love of humanity should mean sacrifice and self-denial; but it was changed into the cheap enjoyment of noble feelings and the easy exercise of a costless idealism. To have utterly degraded love—to have made of love a cover for vapid hearts and lazy minds—to turn love into a refuge for the spiritually indolent and the intellectually insipid—this was the great achievement in religion of the kingdom of complacency!

As the citizens of this kingdom could not endure for themselves the doctrine of their Bible, so they would not allow for their children the shrewd wisdom of Mother Goose. They took quite seriously the recommendation of Plato's *Republic* that, in the ideal society, all the classics of literature, sacred and profane, must be expurgated of any record of conduct unbecoming a lady or a gentleman. What, indeed, would happen to the minds of the little ones if they read such dreadful tales about cruel stepmothers, and bad fairies, and evil-minded witches, and poisoned apples? Here, too, there must be nothing but kindly godfathers, and lyric love potions, and sweet little boys and girls on their very best of behavior.

Accordingly, in the revised version of "Little Red Riding Hood," nothing was said about how the wolf ate her up and how she had to be cut out of his belly by a passing huntsman. No, she managed to escape out of the house in just the nick of time. And, in the modern edi-

tion of "The Three Little Pigs," there was nothing so
sadistic as the wolf's falling down the chimney and
being boiled in a kettle of water. Not at all! The wolf
just jumped up the chimney again and ran for dear life.
So, you see, nobody got hurt no matter what happened—
not Little Red Riding Hood for being a naughty girl;
not the wolf for being cruel and cannibalistic. All they
got out of it was just a bad scare!

The Bible and Mother Goose—Jahweh, God of
Battles, and the Big Bad Wolf—Jesus Christ and Little
Red Riding Hood: all of these were suspect in the cul-
ture of complacency!

## VI

It was Immanuel Kant who remarked that the ability
to experience the sublime is one of the tokens of high
spiritual endowment in man. The earthquake, the storm
at sea, the destruction of war, the volcano in eruption, the
hurricane with its track of devastation—these things do
violence to the will and agitate the imagination, rather
than bring to us the sense of calm and of repose which is
found in the contemplation of beauty. Yet it is in the
presence of such experiences that the nobler type of man
has some glimpse of his "supersensible destination." His
emotional state is a mingling of feelings of fear and of
security. Fear arises from the threat to one's personal
safety, the menace to one's existence as a finite being.
But there is also a wondrous sense of security in that, at

just this moment, man becomes most keenly aware of that part of him which is more than the corruptible body. Now he suddenly realizes that he is also mind and soul, and that there is in him an eternal spirit which cannot be touched by the onslaughts of temporal calamity.

The demoniac is equally at home in the storm and in the tumult. Only, he blends himself with the fury of the forces of nature, rather than discovering that there are in him forces which are mightier than these. Like Lord Byron at Lake Geneva, when he sees the lightning leap from crag to crag, and the dark thunder-clouds gather, and the waters whipped up in white-crested wrath, then he would become a portion of the tempest and a sharer in its fierce and far delight. To this extent, the demonic-man is superior to the swine-man, in that the demoniac is above the fears of the flesh, and appreciates the wild joys of the unleashed spirit as it breaks beyond the bounds of routine and conventional behavior. It is the limitation of the demoniac, however, that he loses himself in the meaningless orgies of the natural passions, and cannot experience the romantic thrill of an aspiration that is spiritual.

According to Kant, it is the mark of the pagan, of the superstitious man, that he experiences only the emotion of fear under these circumstances. He has none of that humility, none of that trustfulness in the purposes of God, which might enable him to find, in these threats to his personal welfare, only the occasion which should set off, in sharper relief, his spiritual meaning. And he has not enough even of primitive animal vitality to take delight in the wild frenzy of natural forces. So it is that the pagan man, the swine-man, knows nothing but terror before the tumults of the sublime. All he can think of is how to protect his comfort and his physical security. The pagan man is Voltaire, in his retreat at *Les Délices* on Lake Geneva, hearing the storm roaring without, and caring only to gather his garments more closely about him, to utter another *bon mot*, and to build up the fire more brightly in the grate. The swine-man is Lucretius hiding behind the wall in his hill-top garden, as he looks down on the battle in the plain below, and thinking only of how pleasant, by contrast, is his own unruffled ease. This is the wisdom of complacency.

Lo, the cowardly and the complacent, the decent and the respectable, the peaceful and the prosperous:

They sit like cats by the fire, warming themselves at the hearth of other men's thoughts and achievements. They have nice, soft paws; only, beware of the claws concealed beneath! They do not bark, nor do they bite: they only spit—and scratch: therein consists their refinement. They are solicitous about little things: therein lies their considerateness and their sensitivity. They do not like strange persons and intruders—nor untoward weather nor wild seasons. They are so home-loving: for them, it is enough to have peace and quiet!

They lick their fine coats and purr softly to themselves, saying—"Consider the perfection of our manners, and the orderliness of our way of living. We do not go bounding about, barking noisily and disturbing the neighbors. Our virtue is to conform well to our environment—that is our good taste! To be harmonious with our surroundings, like any other carefully selected bit of furniture—that is our aspiration! We are the well-bred ones, dainty in our appetites, and polite in our excretions. And we commit no nuisances!"

But should the rains descend, and the floods come, and the winds blow and beat upon the house, till there be left of it neither fire nor fireside—that were no season for hearth-loving tabby cats!

# Four:

# THE RETURN OF
# THE PRODIGAL

*A certain man had two sons: And the younger of them said to his father, Father, give me the portion of goods that falleth to me. And he divided unto them his living.*

*And not many days after the younger son gathered all together, and took his journey into a far country, and there wasted his substance in riotous living. And when he had spent all, there arose a mighty famine in that land; and he began to be in want. And he went and joined himself to a citizen of that country; and he sent him into his fields to feed swine. And he would fain have filled his belly with the husks that the swine did eat: and no man gave unto him.*

*And when he came to himself, he said, How many hired servants of my father's have bread enough and to spare, and I perish with hunger! I will arise and go to my father, and will say unto him, Father, I have sinned against Heaven, and before thee, and am no more worthy to be called thy son: make me as one of thy hired servants.*

*And he arose, and came to his father. But when he was yet a great way off, his father saw him, and had compassion, and ran, and fell on his neck, and kissed him. And the son said unto him, Father, I have sinned against Heaven, and in thy sight, and am no more worthy to be called thy son.*

But the father said to his servants, Bring forth the best robe, and put it on him; and put a ring on his hand, and shoes on his feet: And bring hither the fatted calf, and kill it; and let us eat, and be merry: For this my son was dead, and is alive again; he was lost, and is found.

*Luke. 15:11–24.*

# 4: THE RETURN OF
THE PRODIGAL

It is a fortunate thing for a people when it has a spiritual heritage which, through sheer force of inertia, continues to operate even though contemporary conditions are not congenial to that heritage. With the individual, it is a common experience that habits acquired in early training may continue to function when they have been repudiated by the intellect, and when current fashions might call for an entirely different mode of behavior. With a society, it is the power of tradition and the impetus of ancient *mores* which carry on regardless of present emergencies. Of course, there must be some social agency—political, economic, or ecclesiastical—for implementing the tradition. And often enough a tradition which continues to function simply through the force of inertia may be a cause of retrogression, or of the retarding of significant social development. But, if the spiritual heritage is a heritage of noble ideals, then it will be custom, and not novelty, that makes for growth.

For instance, the social ideals which controlled governmental policy in the United States in the 1930's could not have been a product of the spiritual climate of that decade. Only a naïve economic determinism would think so. That spiritual climate was pretty well reflected in the best-selling novel and most popular motion picture of the time—*Gone With The Wind*. The two principal characters of the novel were a perfect projection of the mood—not of the South after the Civil War—but of the American people after the First World War. Rhett Butler, with his utter cynicism about all ideals, his belief that wars are fought only for money, his frank admiration for a selfishness that is uninhibited by humanitarian sentiments and scarcely veiled by civilized decencies; Scarlett O'Hara, with her forthright and realistic egotism, her rapacity in exploiting all people and events for her own ends—ignorant of honor, untouched by tenderness, unweakened by love: these two persons were an epitome of the prevailing spiritual temper. The mighty oath of Scarlett O'Hara that, whatever other ill might befall her, she would never again be conquered by poverty, was an oath already grimly taken by millions of American people. This novel, indeed, gave eloquent expression to our disillusionment after a war fought to make the world safe for democracy, and to our sense of despair and of defeat in the face of a terrible depression. No time, now, for ideals! One had energy only for the brute struggle for existence—to grab for oneself, and to grab again.

The humanitarian social legislation of the New Deal was not a product of this mood. It was the product of a

more ancient spiritual heritage, the concrete procedures
of which were now apposite to present conditions. And
the government which applied these procedures, while
it answered to the needs of the times, did not respond to
the temper of the times. The spiritual heritage which
now found specific social implementation was a product,
not of ruthless and disillusioned egotists, but of idealists,
who, fully cognizant of the sufferings of their fellow-
men, were nevertheless hopeful of building a society
where there should be life abounding not only in material goods but also in the goods of the mind and of the
soul. It was the patient work of generations of far-
sighted scholars, of prophets of the social gospel, of
heroic crusaders for humanity, which now bore fruit in
the legislation designed to guarantee men freedom from
fear and from want, and to establish them further in the
great civil and religious liberties. To this extent, the
nation under the New Deal was the ungrateful recipient,
from a previous age, of favors which it could never have
devised for itself.

Looking back, now, from the vantage-point of the
early 1940's, we can see that, for the past twenty years,
our country had been enacting the first two stages in the
progress of the prodigal son. In the decade of the twenties, having gathered together all the goods that fell to
us from a rich patrimony, we took our journey into a
country far from our spiritual birthplace, and there
wasted our substance in riotous living. This was a time
for orgiastic rituals in high finance—for fantastic specu-

lations in real estate, for gigantic mergers of corporations, for holding companies that pyramided their way
to heaven like the Tower of Babel. It was a time, too, for
luxurious and careless living, when, of a sooth, men
took no thought for the morrow, saying, What shall we
eat? or What shall we drink? or Wherewithal shall we
be clothed?—being confident that their heavenly Father
knew that they had need of all these things, and that He
could never deny to His chosen people the continued
enjoyment of a material abundance that was more than
Solomon's in all his glory.

But the substance that was wasted in the magnificent
twenties was also a spiritual substance. We could be
done, now, with the old-fashioned taboos of a puritan
morality. Sexual continence of any sort—pre-marital
chastity, even marital fidelity—was an item that could
be easily dispensed with in an enlightened age. Politics
could preserve an external respectability through a president who was the epitome of all the old, homely,
Yankee virtues; but its inner working revealed a frenzy
of graft and of corruption that had not been equalled since
the administration of President Grant. In the conduct of
business, to be sure, one still talked about frugality and
farsightedness; but, when the promise of the future was
so great, frugality was only for fools, and the truly far-
sighted person was the one who capitalized now on what
he knew he would surely earn later on. Religion, of
course, must have its place, but the intelligent man
scarcely believed in God any more; and, even if his lips
repeated the prayers of the Christian faith, his heart

and his mind were those of the humanist and the agnostic.

And, when we had spent all, there arose a mighty famine in the land. The great temple of finance on Wall Street, once the stamping-ground of proud and trampling bulls, was given over as a prey to the bear, whose whelps held in their claws only momentarily a booty that the next instant vanished into thin air. The tilled fields of the nation were destroyed by the drought. The great engines of our factories were terrible in their stillness. The roaring channels of communication quieted down to a thin trickle of goods and services which were most needed only by those who could not afford to buy. And the careless citizens that had once lain, lolling on their ivory divans, dining off fresh lamb and fatted veal, listening to the music of the crooner, and lapping wine by the bowlful, would now fain have filled their bellies with the husks that the swine did eat.

But this famine was also a famine of the spirit. Men could not recover, in depression, the ideals they had cast away in prosperity. They still worshiped Mammon in the decade of the thirties, as they worshiped Mammon in the decade of the twenties; but now it was with the bitterness of those whose prayers are unanswered. Nor could they bear up easily under the chastisements of this god, who had trained them for fatness and for ease, but had not disciplined them for want and for care. Yet, if they did not have prosperity, they did crave security; and, if they could no longer enjoy the reckless abandon of the old-time festivities, they did modestly desire a little fun. To be comfortable, to be secure, to have a little fun: these were the ends of life. As for the challenge of the ideal—well, one could be a pacifist. That, surely, was enough of spiritual aspiration—to wish to be left in peace!

It was this temper of mind which waited at the receiving end of a humanitarian social legislation which was the gift of an entirely different moral outlook. This meeting of the spiritual heritage of the past with the spiritual temper of the moment did, indeed, produce a strange blend. One might believe, of course, that, in the long run, the reforms of the New Deal might lay the foundations of a society which should be richer in the goods of the spirit as well as in the goods of the body. But the immediate effect of this conjunction of the two streams of tendency was the pollution of the great river of idealism that flowed down from the past. What was intended to free men from material wants, so that they might pursue more joyously the goods of the spirit, only resulted in an unseemly scramble for offices, and favors, and pensions, and sinecures, and privileges, which, in themselves, would only bind men more slavishly with the shackles of Mammon. And so the gifts of the spiritual heritage of the past were corrupted as they were received by the spiritual temper of the present.

II

The social reforms of the New Deal are only one illustration of the complexity of the problem of defining the spiritual traditions of a people. In a general sense, those traditions are the body of ideals, good or bad, which are determinative of the conduct of a nation. But it is difficult to know just how to get hold of those ideals, for they are never the automatic reflex of the environment, as the naïve materialist would like to believe.

Certainly geography is not the key to the problem. Geographically, the United States is as close to Mexico as it is to Canada, and closer to much of South America than it is to Europe. But we have more spiritual affinities with Canada than we do with Mexico, and probably more affinities with parts of Europe than we do with most of South America. With the Latin American republics we share a common revolt against the tyrannies and stupidities of the Old World; but their culture is Spanish and Portuguese, while ours is Anglo-Saxon; and their political institutions, while favoring certain ideals of democracy, nevertheless employ the forms of a dictatorship.

Indeed, our deepest spiritual affinities are with nations that are remote from us geographically. There are strong cultural bonds that tie us to Great Britain and to republican France, in spite of the Atlantic Ocean; and there are equally strong bonds that tie us to democratic China, in spite of the still greater Pacific Ocean. The islands of the Philippines are farther removed than the islands of Japan; but the American and the Filipino have a comradeship in the faith in freedom which the American and the Nipponese cannot share together. Yet, if the pseudo-social science of "geopolitics" were permitted to prescribe our foreign policy, we should have to alter radically the direction of our spiritual destiny. To be sure, with those who are next door to us, it is always necessary to be a neighbor, and a good neighbor; but a spiritual brother is still our closest kin even though the high seas lie between us.

It is equally clear that economics is not the clue to the problem. This has been made evident, in recent times, by the varying responses of different countries to the facts of depression and of national bankruptcy. In the face of such a situation, the force of the *mores* in one country makes for a mood of despair and of fatalistic acquiescence; in another country, for violent revolution, with a radical program of reform; in another, for a conservative reaction during which the tyrant and the exploiter only strengthen their hold on power; in a democracy, either for half-hearted adjustments which qualify without eradicating the sources of evil, or for intelligent social experimentation which moves on, without bloodshed, to a better and more humane order of things.

The stupidity of the economic interpretation of ideals was shown conclusively by the failure of the policy of appeasement towards Hitler. Here it was assumed that a few concessions in markets and raw materials, or in *lebensraum* and colonies, would be enough to convert the German eagle into a sucking dove of peace. But, when Hitler took over new territories and new industrial resources, he used them, not to raise the standard of living

RETURN OF THE PRODIGAL 113

of his people and to further them in a career of commerce, but simply to build a larger army, a more potent air force, and a more terrifying secret police. Only if the ideals of Germany had been those of a bourgeois capitalism to begin with would the strategy of economic concessions have been of any effect. But a hungry lion is not converted into a gentle lamb when we throw him an antelope to eat; he is converted only into a stronger and more rapacious lion, ready to devour more antelopes as well as every living thing that may fall in his path. Similarly, it is nothing but materialistic sentimentalism to believe that, in the reconstruction after the war, a full breadbasket will radically alter the *mores* of a people if its spiritual traditions are already those of the wolf, or the jackal, or the pig.

Considerations of race are of still less help than economic considerations. Switzerland is an ancient example of how a people may be held together by a common spiritual heritage in spite of sharp differences of race, of language, and even of general culture. Here is a republic which has three official languages—German, Italian, French—for the transaction of all governmental business, and which harbors in its borders persons who look to several other nations for their traditions in literature, philosophy, and art. Yet the Swiss are held together by common loyalties to the ideals of their own country. With this example before us—not to mention the United States—it is a wonder that we ever paid any attention to the Nazi claim of a right to incorporate all persons of

Germanic descent into one political state. For it is not the racial stock which makes up the unity of a state, but the set of ideals to which its people give allegiance. In a democracy, it does not matter—or should not matter—whether we have Jew or Gentile, male or female, colored or white—but all are one through their faith in the ideals of liberty, and justice, and fraternity. Likewise, in fascism, with regard to those who are eligible for membership in its ranks, it matters not whether we have Nordic, or Oriental, or Latin, or American, whether one speaks German, or Japanese, or Italian, or English: all are made one through their faith in their führer and through the belief that it is might alone which makes right.

In a day when political institutions carry increasing weight, one might expect to find in them the bearer of a nation's spiritual heritage. But political institutions do not stand by themselves. This was illustrated by the League of Nations, and by the short-lived German Republic after the First World War. As a political device, the League of Nations probably had more merits than defects. Unfortunately the people in its member groups did not ardently cherish the ideals for which the League stood, with the result that the whole mechanism soon fell into innocuous desuetude. The same was true of the German Republic. It is only part of the story to say that German democracy was destroyed by lack of cooperation from the democracies of Britain, France, and America. The other part of the story is that the Germans themselves never accepted the ideals of democracy, and so began to sabotage the experiment from the beginning. The mere fact that they had political institutions that were democratic was worthless in the face of a profoundly anti-democratic spiritual heritage which still glorified the strong man in politics, looked up to the military profession as the highest social caste, and preferred the efficiency of regimentation to the uncertainties of liberty and of growth.

It is also clear that the spiritual heritage that we call democratic does not depend primarily on democratic political institutions, and that it can function effectively in a great variety of forms of government. The democracy that is in the United States, or in Great Britain, does not depend solely upon the political forms that obtain in those countries. Rather is it rooted in the ancient *mores* of the people, *mores* which, for us, long antedate the actual framing of the Constitution, or the Jeffersonian, or Jacksonian revolutions. It is not materially impaired, either, by the fact that, in the United States, the *mores* put more emphasis upon social equality, while, in England, they allow more distinctions of caste. The political institutions of China, moreover, might be said to be radically undemocratic. They are an expression of that enlightened, benevolent despotism which Voltaire hoped to find in the potentates of Europe, but which, apparently, can be realized only in a strange oriental blend of the war-lord, the Christian, and the mandarin. Yet it would not be too inaccurate to say that, at this moment, the genuine spirit of democracy probably stirs more deeply among the people of China than it does in the well-established democracies of the Occident.

Finally, it is clear that the ideals of a people are not a direct reflex of the stage at which they stand in the enjoyment of the fruits of science and of technology. This is evident enough when we examine the case of the individual. Let us suppose that there are two persons in a community who drive the same make of car, who live in homes equally furnished with modern conveniences, who call on the same sort of doctors when they are sick, the same plumbers and electricians when their houses are in need of repair, and the same sort of dieticians and physical culturists to keep them in good health. But one may be a good citizen, and the other fellow a gangster. One may be drawing on the resources of science and of technology to perfect himself and his family in spiritual growth, and to contribute his bit toward the social betterment of his country. The other man is using science and technology to further his own selfish ends, and to destroy all the values of the civilization in which he lives.

The same can be true of a nation. It is a gross illusion to believe that the spread, all over the earth, of a technological culture will bring mankind into spiritual unity. As Reinhold Niebuhr repeatedly observes, in his *Reflections on the End of an Era*, it is a distinguished mark of our times that we are mechanically united and spiritually divided. The fact is that science and technology are only tools. They can be, and are, the tools of fascism as well as of democracy, of anti-Christ as well as of a Christian culture. It may be that, ideally, the spirit of science is most compatible with a humane and a liberal civilization. But, in the past, autocracies have found ways to keep alive the scientific spirit and method for a privileged few, while the great masses were deprived of the benefits; and we have no warrant for believing that, in the future, a nation should be unable to exploit science only for its own ends, and as an instrument to tyrannize over people rather than to free them.

From this analysis one might be tempted to conclude that the spiritual heritage of a people is like the wind, which bloweth whither it listeth, and cannot be caught in a net, nor lured into a snare. But a set of ideals which had no rootage in concrete institutions would be as useless, as a set of ideals which was nothing but a reflex of economic conditions would be meaningless. What we are forbidden to believe is any naïve monism which should link our ideals only with this, or only with that, material circumstance. The probability remains that our spiritual heritage has various connections with factors that are political, economic, geographic, racial, and technological; but that the connection with no one of these is indispensable; and that the relationship between the two is always a reciprocal one of give and take. Such a view is in accord with a pluralistic rendering of history. But we are also led on to the conclusion that, once a spiritual tradition has had its genesis and has established itself in the *mores* of a people, then, to some extent, it leads an autonomous existence, developing its own implications without regard to specific material instrumentalities. Spiritual values are as real as economic conditions; and ideals exist as truly in nature as the mechanisms through which they get expression.

### III

Modern history since the Renaissance is the story of a civilization which has been doubtful of the reality of ideals. It is a civilization which has developed brilliantly the techniques—political, economic, and technological—by which men live, and has simply taken it for granted that ideals are an automatic reflex of these techniques. It is this which, in a rough way, marks the difference between classical-medieval culture and modern culture. The contrast can be pointed up by comparing the theories of knowledge and the social utopias entertained by Plato and by Francis Bacon.

Plato had a theory of knowledge, but he was not altogether an epistemologist in the modern sense. For the basic problem, as he defined it, was, not how do we know, but what is worth knowing. It is ends that are worth knowing, not means—the "why" and the "whereto" of life rather than the "how." Who understands a lyre? Who understands a ship? The modern man, a Baconian, would reply: the craftsman understands the lyre, and the engineer understands the ship.

Plato would reply: only the musician understands the lyre, because he knows the purpose for which it is designed; only the pilot understands the ship, because he knows the harbor to which it must be guided. The knowledge of making is inferior to the knowledge of use and of enjoyment. The knowledge of means and mechanisms is subordinate to the knowledge of goals, values, purposes.

Hence Plato displays a contempt for facts which is scandalous to the empirically-minded modern man. In the celebrated metaphor of the Cave, he suggests that the hard-headed practical man, with his shabby emotions, his meretricious knowledge, his cheap worldly wisdom, lives only in a world of shadows. Only those who have glimpsed the light of the ideal have any comprehension of reality. It is true also that the Children of Light, by virtue of the heavenly vision, are made unfit for worldly conversations, and appear ridiculous when they turn their hands to the trivial arts and skills of a mundane existence. More than this, they are persecuted and crucified because of their divine discontent with the ignoble order of facts and of actualities. For the Children of Darkness hate the Children of Light.

Francis Bacon, the great seer of modern civilization, was a Child of Darkness unashamed. In the classical-medieval heritage of values, he could see nothing but laborious cobwebs of learning which might be admirable for the fineness and the thread of the work, but which were of no substance nor profit. The apostles of the ideal were apt at argument, but barren of works; and the only fruit of their inquiries was monstrous altercations and barking questions. Now, at last, we should learn how to do things, and not be troubled overmuch with what was worth doing. "The end of our foundation is the knowledge of causes, and secret motions of things; and the enlarging of the bounds of human empire to the effecting of all things possible." Causes, not consequences; origins, not functions; mechanisms, not values: these are what is worth knowing. Indeed, it is only the knowledge of means that gives meaning to life.

The utopias of the two thinkers embody the same scheme of values that is reflected in their epistemologies. Plato's *Republic* is a pattern of the ideal—a pattern laid up in heaven, beholding which we may organize our lives accordingly. It matters not that the *Republic* does not exist, and may never exist, any more than it matters that the artist's portrait of the perfect human figure is not a copy of fact. For man lives, not by sordid facts, but by the inspiration of the ideal. The perennial issues of life are, not the mechanical ones, but the problems of justice, wisdom, courage, and temperance. How to find rulers with wisdom; how to have citizens who are courageous in their loyalty to the law; how to have men who are temperate in the enjoyments of the flesh and in the pursuits of commerce; how to build the just state: if we are to be concerned with any mechanisms at all, then the only mechanisms that matter are those that implement these values.

The mind of Francis Bacon—this "wisest, brightest, meanest of mankind"—was singularly untroubled by such scruples. His personal career was a reflection of the ambivalence of his own utopia and of the whole of modern civilization. For he was wise and bright in his understanding of the mechanisms of life, and mean and ignoble in his grasp of the ends of life. In his *New Atlantis*, the central institution is Solomon's House. It is a technologist's paradise. Here, with the benefit of experimental laboratories, research scholarships, traveling fellowships, there go on great scientific investigations in mining, in metallurgy, in zoölogical studies, in pharmacopoeia, in telegraphy and telephony and in submarine navigation, and in the development of improved bakeries, and breweries, and fertilizers, and cosmetics. But precious little time is wasted on justice, wisdom, courage, and temperance, or on faith, and hope, and love. This is, indeed, the utopia of the ethically infantile modern man.

It is significant that today we continue to read Plato's *Republic*, but that we turn to Bacon's *New Atlantis* only with an antiquarian's interest. For the teaching of the *Republic* is a statement of the problems in the eternal quest of man for the life that is truly abundant. On the other hand, the prophecies of the *New Atlantis*—remarkable as they were at the time they were written—have all been fulfilled. We have brought into being —far beyond Bacon's expectations—the reality of his technologist's paradise. But what has it profited the modern man that he should have gained this whole world, and, at the same time, should have lost his own soul!

The difference between Francis Bacon and Plato is the difference between science and religion. As we sail our ship over the seas of this life, we need an engineer to manage the motors, and a pilot to plot the course. Science is the engineer; religion is the pilot. Without an engineer, our ship is becalmed on the waters, or drifts helplessly with every tide or current. Without a pilot, our ship is foundered on hidden rocks and shoals, and cannot find the harbor. Science is an abstraction of those aspects of reality which lend instrumental efficacy to our knowledge. Religion is an abstraction of those aspects of reality which reveal its meanings and consummations. The one is concerned with means and with mechanisms; the other with ends and with ideals.

If there is a conflict between science and religion, then it is partly justified, and partly unjustified. It is unjustified when the pilot steps down into the engine-room, and tries to manage the motors. He knows nothing about it; and his true place is in the pilot-house. It is unjustified when the engineer steps up on the bridge, and tries to plot the course. He knows nothing about it; and his true place is in the engine-room. But there is an inevitable, and a fruitful, interaction between science and religion, insofar as the inventions of the engineer may make possible the plotting of new courses hitherto untraversed, and insofar as the aspiration of the pilot after new harbors may call forth the devising of new mechanisms the need of which was not till then recognized. There is, moreover, a reciprocal discipline which the one exercises upon the other, in that the pilot has his own mechanisms the construction of which may call for some of the wisdom of the engineer; and any progress in the devices of the engine-room may make possible a variety of new courses of travel the value of which must be in part judged in the pilot-house.

If this much be granted, then common sense will be prompt to nod its head sagely, and to remark that, of course, we need both science and religion. Either one without the other makes for significant weakness in the structure of a civilization. Mechanism alone dehumanizes. Mechanism alone is the horrors of the early stages of the industrial revolution. It is the scandal of a civilization which employs its science and its technology as much in the destructive work of war as in the constructive arts of peace. It is the spiritual torpor of a people which cares only for comfort, prosperity, and complacency, and which can see no higher goal for the individual than that he should attain the status of a well fed, well scrubbed prize pig.

Idealism alone enervates. It is true, as Bacon said, that the pure idealists are like children—prompt to prattle, but barren of works. The pure mechanists, on the other hand, are abounding in business, but unilluminated by meaning. Yet because the idealist disdains the dirty business of life, because he cannot drag himself down from the lofty contemplation of pure essences to the degrading manipulation of mere facts, his visions, so far as the people of this world are concerned, are too often of beautiful but ineffectual angels beating in the void their luminous wings in vain. It is a sweet dream to see oneself, as with the wings of such an angel, traversing the clear empyrean, unhampered by clod of flesh or foot of clay; but here, on this earth, it is enough of an accomplishment if we can walk and not be weary, can run and not faint.

However, if it is true, in general, that we need both science and religion, it is never true, in particular, that we stand equally in need of science and of religion at a given moment. Indeed, that phase of civilization which historians have called "modern" is a phase in which we have developed science abundantly but have scarcely turned our attention to religion. We need to worry no longer about the vision of Francis Bacon: we have fulfilled it. But we do need to turn once more to the vision of Plato, and of the gospels: for this vision is not only unfulfilled; it has been forgotten.

IV

If we consider in detail the ingredients that go to make up the spiritual *gestalt* of the American people, we shall find a commingling of elements that are ideal and of elements that are more instrumental in character. Unquestionably a social Christianity is one of the most important features in the heritage. The concern of early

Pilgrims and Puritans, and even of Quakers and Baptists and Methodists, with doctrinal issues should never blind us to the fact that theological doctrine, for them, had a very definite relevance to the kind of society they were trying to establish on this earth. They were the modern bearers of the impulse of medieval Christendom to order the world in terms of its rôle as a place of preparation for a higher human destiny. Of course, their bias was Protestant rather than Catholic, somewhat more individualistic than corporative, and favoring the teachings of the Old Testament or of the first century of church history, rather than the accumulated wisdom of the entire Christian tradition. But this meant, anyway, that they retained some of the prophetic passion for social justice; that, according to their own lights, they had a sense of the sacredness of personality; and that they never forgot that life has a higher meaning than might be revealed in its material circumstances.

Another ingredient in our spiritual *gestalt* is the heritage of the ideals of political democracy. I say, the ideals of political democracy, rather than its mechanisms. This meant a regard for the values of life, liberty, fraternity, equality, justice, property, and the pursuit of happiness. In part, this heritage was secular and anti-clerical, and, in part, it was explicitly linked with Christian teachings. In any case, most of these values—except, perhaps, the last two—were inherently congenial to Christian tradition. It is true that the mechanisms by which these values were implemented varied greatly from one primitive

American community to the other, but not till modern times did the American people become so immersed in these mechanisms that they no longer understood the purposes these mechanisms were supposed to serve.

But the American is not only a Christian and a democrat; he is also a business man. Our political heritage might stress the great civil liberties, but our economic heritage emphasized the liberty of *laissez-faire*. Business activity was found compatible with the rest of our tradition, because our Protestantism and our political democracy, as well as our interest in business, were part of the complex of a middle-class culture. In the early stages of our history, it was possible for the religious and the political elements to hold the upper hand over the business element. But, at a time beginning roughly with the Civil War and running down to the end of the 1920's, it may be said that business activity became the dominant element in the tradition, and reduced both religion and politics to functions that were purely ancillary to profit-making. Religion provided a sanction, and politics gave protection. But the real values and meanings of life were now found in the realm of economic activity.

The fourth ingredient in our heritage is science and technology. So far as science involves the cultivation of the scientific spirit in all human relations, it may be said to be an ideal value. But, for most Americans, science is simply technology. It is the results of applied science in promoting human comfort and well-being that really hold our attention. In any case, it cannot be sufficiently emphasized that the faith in science and in technology is a basic ingredient in our spiritual *gestalt*. The United States is, perhaps, the only great nation in history that literally grew up with the Industrial Revolution. At every fresh stage in the advance of our empire on this continent, when we needed new tools for opening up unexplored areas, or for exploiting natural resources, there the tools were, providentially placed in our hands, ready for immediate use. So it is that our people are as handy at a machine-shop as they are at a revival meeting; and, while leaders in politics and in business may command our primary, practical loyalty, our most exalted hero-worship is for the genius in technology and invention. We may loyally follow a Roosevelt, or even a Rockefeller; but we worship before an Edison, or a Henry Ford.

Pervading these four elements in our spiritual heritage, there have been, in the past, two qualities which have distinguished our moral character. One of these qualities was idealism. It was idealism of a rather practical and sentimental sort. It might express itself somewhat crassly in the faith of the business man that he could forever go on discovering new economic opportunities and making still greater profits, or in the faith of the technologist that he could work a revolution in our manner of living with a new Ford, or a synthetic silk stocking, or another vitamin pill. In politics it was revealed in a persistent strain of utopianism which expected that democracy could soon be made a concrete social reality; and, in religion, it meant the firm belief that the Kingdom of God, like prosperity, must be just around the corner. The sophisticated expression of this mood is found, significantly enough, in the writings of our two greatest American philosophers—in William James' doctrine of the "will-to-believe," and in John Dewey's confidence in "creative intelligence." In any case, this mood is the polar opposite of cynicism, defeatism, and disillusionment. It is a mood which believes that something can be done about it. It is the faith that human character and human intelligence, cooperating with the beneficent impulses of nature, or with the just laws of an almighty God, can bring society progressively along the road to a state of affairs more rich in the blessings of the spirit and in the comforts of the body. Certainly it has been this quality of idealism, both sentimental and practical, which has caused the older and more weary nations of the earth to look to the United States with high hopes and expectations.

But the other pervasive quality has been equally important. It was the quality of discipline. The best generic name for this tradition of discipline is Puritanism, if one understands Puritanism in its creative, rather than in its decadent, phases. The average American today may find it rather comical to be told that he is a Puritan; but it is significant that almost all European visitors to this country immediately single out Puritanism as a distinguishing trait of our culture. Its roots in our moral and religious heritage are obvious. Its relationship to our economic virtues has been clarified by writers like Weber, Tawney, and Richard Niebuhr. The money-making business man has been a man of Puritan virtues; and it is noteworthy that the families of our great plutocracy which hold on best to their fortunes are often those—like the Rockefellers, for instance—which rigorously adhere to their Puritan heritage. The connection of Puritan disciplines with our political pattern may not be so obvious, but it is highlighted in figures like Abraham Lincoln and Woodrow Wilson. Finally, the American scientist in his laboratory, whether inventing a new gadget, or discovering a new truth, displays an austere dedication to duty which is worthy of the descendant of the Pilgrim Fathers.

What has happened in recent times to this four-fold heritage, with its two pervasive qualities, can be seen at a glance. In the first place, there has been a systematic corrosion of the qualities of discipline and of idealism within the culture of complacency. As the worship of Mammon has taken the place of devotion to Christ, there has been substituted, for the old, austere respect for spiritual personality, a new individualism that is selfish, sentimental, and materialistic. An educational procedure, alleged to be progressive, but, in fact, retrogressive, has conspired with political apathy, economic rapacity, moral indolence, and religious sentimentalism, to replace idealism with cynicism and sophistication, and to break down self-discipline into a self-expression that is as inane as it is impotent. But of this enough has already been said.

The second important change has been that the means have usurped the place of the ends. In other words, economic activity has gained the dominant position, and has enslaved religion, politics, and technology to its uses. Thus it is that we have come to prefer the politician to the political scientist and the statesman; the business entrepreneur and the profiteer to the designer of a just economic order; the successful parson of "practical Christianity" to the prophet of the gospel. In our disregard of the significant goals and purposes of life, we have been like the unruly crew, in Plato's ship, that dismissed the pilot as a useless star-gazing babbler, and decided to run the vessel itself. We have cared more for the polished brass on our boat than for the course that was charted for it; and we have been so intoxicated with the roar of her mighty engines, that we were reckless of where they might carry us. "We don't know where we're going, but we're on our way!" This popular phrase of a decade or so ago, uttered, not in a mood of melancholy and despair, but with all the zest of wild abandon to the mere exhibition of energy, was a measure of our moral idiocy.

Undoubtedly the New Deal marked the initiation of a phase in our history during which the political once more shall gain ascendancy over the economic. Within limits, too, it meant a fresh consideration of the problem of the ends of life, or, at least, of the meaning of democracy. Herbert Hoover was the last great representative of the old order, as Franklin D. Roosevelt has been the inaugurator of the new. If Hoover was an engineer, then Roosevelt is a pilot. One may charge against each one a deficiency in the virtues of the other. Herbert Hoover, although he has always been an intelligent political thinker, has usually been content to give formal elaboration to ends that were already taken for granted, and has distinguished himself chiefly in the passion for the efficient administration of his business. Conversely, against Franklin D. Roosevelt, the accusation may be brought, that he has not cared too much for efficiency and for economy—the virtues of the engineer. Whether or not he is a good pilot of our ship of state is a judgment that must be further clarified by subsequent history. Some persons may think that his manœuverings have been more noteworthy for brilliance and for dexterity, than for sense of purpose. Others may believe, with this writer, that, in view of the heavy seas encountered, he has steered a remarkably straight course.

But the simple restoration of political idealism to American life will not be enough to complete our spiritual reconstruction. The social reforms of the New Deal may be vitiated as have been the educational reforms of John Dewey. They may be engulfed and smothered in the vast slough of spiritual despond which is the culture of complacency. Political devices are no substitute for religious disciplines; nor are political ideals as adequate as religious values. We shall not be born again, as a peo-

ple, until the theology of Mammon has been supplanted
by the theology of Christ.

v

At church conventions which are called to discuss the
bases of a just and durable peace, it is customary to have
one section on politics, another on economics, and a third
on the spiritual aspects. But, while the halo of the honor-
ific goes to the third topic, it is the first two that command the attention of practical thinkers. And, though
the political and economic bases of peace may be discussed in detail and with precision, we are usually content with pious platitudes and with sentimental effusions
on the subject of spiritual reconstruction. It is, indeed, a
measure of our spiritual blindness that, within the church
itself, we should have such vague notions about the
meaning of the domain which is considered distinctively
religious.

Yet the problem of spiritual reconstruction is not a
vague one; and the chances are that, in the long run, it
will be the most crucial phase in the re-ordering of the
society of nations. The basic strategy to be followed, although exceedingly complicated in execution, can be
clearly defined. It is: that, in the conquered nations, we
should attempt to revive those elements in their native
traditions which are compatible with a democratically
ordered world; that, in the victorious nations, we should
see to it that the Christian and democratic elements in

their traditions shall take an unequivocal preponderance over elements that are not so ideal. The instrumentalities of this reconstruction may be political, economic, ecclesiastical, and broadly cultural. But no amount of change in political and economic mechanisms will be of any avail unless it is pointed toward, and supported by, a fundamental reconstruction of ideals and values.

For instance, the Nazi state in Germany today is supported by ancient elements in the spiritual heritage of the German people. These are the traditions of the glorification of the military caste; of devotion to a führer, be it a Frederick the Great, or a Bismarck, or an Adolf Hitler; of belief in the racial superiority of the Nordic, or Aryan, peoples; of giving supremacy to the interests of the state, not only over business interests, but even over the claims of the church, the family, and the fine arts. All of these elements are at least one hundred and fifty years old in the German heritage. But there are other elements in the German tradition, at present submerged. There is the old Germany of Martin Luther, and of staunch Protestant piety; the Germany of the skilled craftsman and of the self-respecting burgher, who quietly go about their duties as citizens and business men and fathers of families; the Germany of scholars and of universities, of philosophers, artists, scientists, musicians, theologians, to whom came the whole world that it might sit at their feet. The task of spiritual reconstruction is to bring these submerged elements to the fore again, until they preponderate over the elements now dominant.

In the case of Japan, the realist will have to admit that the problem is more difficult. Here one encounters the same apotheosis of the state, in the form of emperor-worship; the same exaltation of a military caste of Samurai, with its Bushido code of feudal ethics; the same passionate conviction of racial superiority and of special national destiny. Unfortunately, this tradition in Japan is more than one hundred and fifty years old; it is thousands of years old: and, as a natural, indigenous growth, it has a grip on the people that cannot be matched by the more synthetic fascism of Germany. Moreover, Japan has no great tradition of free science and of free philosophy; Christianity has never been too potent an influence in that country; and even the pacifistic religion of Buddhism, in its Zen variant, has been sucked into service to the military ideal. It is conceivable, of course, that a Christian minority might rise to a significant position of political leadership in Japan, as it has in China. In any case, the strategy of spiritual reconstruction in that country will have to be many-sided. It will involve the encouragement of Buddhist and of Christian elements as against the Shinto cult; the attempt to revive the glories of the brief movement of social and political liberalism of a few decades ago; and the pitting of the ideals of a peaceful proletariat and of a peaceful bourgeoisie against the ideals of the Samurai.

It is interesting to note that, among the nations which

we intend to be the victors, China is probably the most firmly set on the way to spiritual reconstruction. This is true, in large measure, because, in spite of the revolution, the Chinese have held onto those elements in their tradition which are essentially democratic: the respect for learning, and for the educated man in public office; a primary interest in the peaceful pursuits of commerce and of the arts; an old habit of *laissez-faire* and of local autonomy in matters political and economic, conjoined with arts of community enterprise and of cooperative effort. The spirit of the Chinese people, moreover, has gone through a longer ordeal by fire than has the spirit of any other nation now at war, and there has been time for the dross to be purged away. Nor is it of little importance that the ruling family of China and other persons in official position are permeated with a genuine Christian idealism which puts to shame the leaders and the peoples of the so-called Christian nations. Here, indeed, in old Cathay, there are the makings of a civilization which shall be as great in its achievements of the mind and of the soul as in its ornaments of the flesh.

Russia offers the peculiar paradox of a nation which is democratic in its ideals, but autocratic in its methods. She stands with one foot on the totalitarian side of the fence, and with the other foot on the democratic side of the fence. Undoubtedly the achievements of communist Russia in social justice and in the moral re-awakening of its people are great as seen against the background of Tzarist Russia. And, since there was no powerful liberal tradition to exploit in the work of the Russian social revolution, it was necessary to be tough and relentless to a degree that could not be comprehended by the democracies. But, while Russia has learned something of justice, she has yet to learn something of liberty and of love. It may be that the Anglo-American peoples can teach Russia something about liberty, but it is a question whether they are fit to teach her anything about love. Probably the ideal strategy for the situation is a reciprocal one, in which we try to get from Russia a fresh vitality in our passion for social justice, and attempt to show her that liberty and love are part of the values and the methods of democracy.

The spiritual rebirth of Great Britain must be, in some respects, analogous to that of the United States. It calls for the Tory tradition's giving way to the democratic tradition. In both countries, this is the fundamental precondition to any real spiritual bond between the Anglo-American peoples. Speaking only from our own point of view, we may say that there is an England which Americans can love and trust. It is the England of the common man, the England that was the cradle of our own liberties, the England that fought bravely on the beaches at Dunkerque and that stood gallantly under the hail of bombs over London. Of course, Americans can admire a Winston Churchill. His stout heart and his indomitable will are something that is beyond class and caste. But, while Americans may admire his courage and his vigor, they may hope, like some Englishmen, that he will be the last great leader to arise from the ranks of the conservatives.

On the other hand, Americans will have to understand that the spiritual rebirth of the British people will follow the more devious routes that are appropriate to a more complex and a more ancient culture. We need to remember that, while, in our own country, we speak of capital and of labor, in England there are capital, and labor, and landed gentry. Some of the great advances in social legislation, curiously enough, have come from the landed gentry—the Tory socialists. At the present moment, moreover, two of the greatest leaders of liberal social reform in England—the Archbishop of Canterbury and the Archbishop of York—belong to an institution which we should regard as the very stronghold of conservatism, namely, the established church.

Finally, the political methodology of the British is expressed, not in the experimental pragmatism of a James and a Dewey, but in the empiricism of a Locke and a Burke. Locke is the spokesman of a liberal empiricism, and Burke of a conservative empiricism. Yet each expresses, in philosophy, the policy of "blundering through" which is supposed to be characteristic of British politics. This policy rests on a realization that the best laid plans of mice and of men "gang aft agley," and hence distrusts any formal rationalism that prescribes with too much precision, or any scientific government that orders with too much efficiency. There are loose ends in the course of history as there are in the lives of individual men. So the best program for progress is one that achieves efficiency by deliberately allowing for a little inefficiency; which values liberty, and therefore, inconsistency, as much as coherence and regimentation; and which cherishes an organic contact with the past, as well as a taste for the growing edge of the future.

But, whatever may be the case with other countries, it is our primary responsibility to set our own house in order. It is time, indeed, that the Prodigal should return to his Father's home. We have been living haphazardly on a four-fold spiritual patrimony—of faith in Christianity, in political democracy, in free enterprise in business, and in science and technology. All of these things are a part of our spiritual heritage, in the objective sense, because, at one time or another, each one of them has been set up as the chief end of life. But, if we are to speak normatively rather than descriptively, then only two of these elements are rightfully entitled to pre-eminence as spiritual forces. These are the faith in Christianity, and the faith in the ideals of political democracy. Henceforth, these values must control the values of business and of technology. Never again, for instance, dare we love a country like China with our Christian and democratic part, while we sell munitions of war to Japan with our industrial part. Undoubtedly new discoveries in business and in technology may have an expanding and reconstructing effect upon the values of Christianity and of democracy. Nevertheless, in the long run, it must be the values that are called spiritual which preponderate over values that are called material. Liberty, justice, and fraternity are more than profits and fat purses; and faith, hope, and love are more than factories, good highways, and electrical appliances.

Such an aspiration does not deny the hope of John Dewey that some day the scientific spirit may be infused into the methods and attitudes of our social institutions. So far as science, as distinguished from simple technology, is a genuine part of our spiritual heritage, there is every likelihood that this fusion can be effected. The patience, the humility, and the tentativeness that belong to the scientific spirit can blend with the patience, the humility, and the childlike open-mindedness that belong to the Christian spirit; and the experimental procedures of science can blend into the customs of compromise, of rational adjustment, and of orderly progress that belong to the methods of a democracy. But, apart from the habit of cooperation among scholars and investigators, there is nothing in the scientific spirit which really makes for love, for social justice, and for effective fraternity between all men; and, for this reason, the contribution of the scientific spirit will be primarily that of a rational supplement to the great values of democracy and of Christianity.

In any case, let us make sure that, no matter how mighty our motors, or how skilful our engineers, our course shall still be charted by pilots who can read the stars.

*Five:*

# THE SUFFERING
# SERVANT OF THE LORD

*Behold my servant, whom I uphold; mine elect, in whom
my soul delighteth; I have put my spirit upon him: he shall
bring forth judgment to the Gentiles. He shall not cry, nor
lift up, nor cause his voice to be heard in the street. A bruised
reed shall he not break, and the smoking flax shall he not
quench: he shall bring forth judgment unto truth. He shall not
fail nor be discouraged, till he have set judgment in the earth:
and the isles shall wait for his law* . . .*

*Isaiah 42:1–4.*

*He is despised and rejected of men; a man of sorrows, and
acquainted with grief: and we hid as it were our faces from
him; he was despised, and we esteemed him not. Surely he hath
borne our griefs, and carried our sorrows: yet we did esteem
him stricken, smitten of God, and afflicted. But he was
wounded for our transgressions, he was bruised for our iniquities: the chastisement of our peace was upon him; and with his
stripes we are healed* . . .*

*Isaiah 53:3–5.*

*He shall see of the travail of his soul, and shall be satisfied:
by his knowledge shall my righteous servant justify many; for
he shall bear their iniquities. Therefore will I divide him a
portion with the great, and he shall divide the spoil with the
strong; because he hath poured out his soul unto death* . . .*

*Isaiah 53:11–12.*

141

# 5:

## THE SUFFERING
## SERVANT OF
## THE LORD

ANY people worth its salt is concerned
with the problem of its national destiny. The absence of
such a concern is evidence of one of two things. Either
that people is living on a primitive level of pagan culture
where it finds complete satisfaction in the daily round of
animal achievements, and remains oblivious of the
trends of time and of the forces of history; or else that
people is living off the proceeds of a rich civilization already attained, and is unwilling to have its comfort disturbed by efforts at further progress. But a people that is
alive is a patriotic people, with a sense of its national
mission in the world.

If, in the past two decades, patriotism was not a fash-
ionable thing in the United States, it was because the
vital impulse in our civilization had fallen into a coma.
Many persons, of course, will protest such a statement—
not because of the suggestion of our spiritual coma—
they are at home in that!—but because it has been a
ritual expression of recent liberal criticism that the American people suffered from an excess of patriotism. However, anyone who bothers to make a relative judgment,

based on a comparison with other nations on the earth, will be struck by the extraordinary absence of patriotic sentiment in this country during the two decades of peace. The fact that, during that time, this sentiment was chiefly exploited by selfish patrioteers was evidence of the low estate into which it had fallen. This does not mean that, when, as now, an emergency arises, the American people cannot be patriotic, and suffer and sacrifice to the last denier and to the last drop of blood. They can; they do; they will—far beyond the expectations of those who understand no other motives than profit and pelf.

But there were good reasons—sound, if not altogether admirable—why the sentiment of patriotism had lapsed in this country. In part, it was due to the historic illusion of isolation, and to the realization that, even in this hemisphere, there was no nation predatory enough or powerful enough to desire, or to be able, to harm us. But still more it was due to the bourgeois illusion that one serves best the public interest by pursuing his private gain. Indeed, the presumed idealism which rejected patriotism as a form of national selfishness was simply a cloak for a more vicious form of personal selfishness in which each individual hoped to be untroubled by national issues, so that he could the more single-heartedly pursue his own narrow ends. The lapse of the patriotic sentiment was of a piece with the lapse of the religious sentiment, because neither for God nor for country did men wish to expend the energies which might more profitably be directed to their own selfish uses.

In this respect, the historic connections between religious enthusiasm and patriotic feeling are instructive. For religion has exploited patriotism as often as patriotism has exploited religion. Moses and Mohammed are two instances of the former case. Both of them found their people divided by narrow tribal loyalties and by distinctions of caste and of function, and exploited the patriotic sentiment to break down these barriers, and to bind them into a more inclusive loyalty. It is true that the Jahweh of Moses was a national deity, and that the Allah of Mohammed became a racial and a cultural deity; but both gods served to carry people beyond the limits of allegiance to self and to family to an allegiance where there was more ample scope for social vision and for selfless living.

To this degree, patriotism is still the handmaiden to the larger ends of high religion in the modern world. Certainly this sentiment deserves much of the credit for the spiritual awakening of the people of China. The Chinese, in the enjoyment of the fruits of an age-old civilization, had become as unpatriotic and quite as selfishly individualistic as had the American people for a while. It was national disaster and national need that brought them to a rediscovery of spiritual values, and of a morality which is more than profit and cheat and chisel. Patriotism also did much to create the spiritual rebirth in Russia, at the manifestations of which we so marvel at this moment. Communism, like the religion of Allah, may have stood for a brotherhood of men beyond national boundaries; but its first task in Russia was to fill out that sense of brotherhood as far as the bounds of the nation. Moreover, it is almost inconceivable how any other sentiment than the patriotic should ever be strong enough to break down the barriers of caste, of religion, and of local political loyalties which divide the people of India. If India gets independence from Britain, then it may be that, like the United States, she will have to go through a terrible civil war to confirm the loyalty to the nation which is higher than these lesser loyalties. For, while Gandhi may have in his hands an effective strategy against British rule, it does not yet appear that he has a strategy which can remove the domestic divisions consuming his people.

## II

The real ethical problem is, not to eliminate patriotism, but to control the ideals to which it is committed. If we are alive as a people, then we must have our sense of national destiny. The point of attention should be the direction in which that national destiny is supposed to move.

Those who are appreciative of the Christian element in the American spiritual heritage may properly be concerned to derive some guidance from that part of our tradition. But there is a tremendous initial difficulty in applying to the United States the national ideals which the prophets developed for Palestine. The land of Palestine was small, while the United States is great in geographic spread. The Israelites were a persecuted and abused minority group among the great nations of their day, but we have been wealthy, and prosperous, and powerful beyond the experience of any other people on the earth. To the absolutist, these differences are no impediment to a literal following, on our part, of the Biblical ideals. But those of a more empirical temper are minded to take these differences into account.

The wide divergence in the methods of approach, in this respect, of the absolutist and the pragmatist is illustrated in the issue of pacifism. The absolutist sees no reason why the United States should not follow the pacifist strategy which Jesus apparently recommended to his own people. The pragmatist sees in such a program, adopted by the American people, an ironical perversion of the teachings of Jesus, a grotesque and blasphemous adherence to the letter of the law in violation of its true spirit. Pacifism is understandable as a strategy for a subject nation like India; and it would be understandable as a strategy for small nations like Denmark, Holland, Belgium, and Greece. But when the most wealthy and powerful nation in the world plays the pacifist—a nation which, by an earlier display of force, might have averted conflict, and which now is in a position, through the use of force, to tip the balance on the side of justice rather than tyranny—when such a nation plays the pacifist, then pacifism looks too much like an excuse for cowardice, for irresponsibility, and for sodden complacency in selfish satisfactions.

Again, it is a problem to know just how the American people can follow that greatest of all national ideals in literature—the ideal of the Suffering Servant of the Lord in *Deutero-Isaiah*. Certainly, it cannot be said of us that we grew up as a root out of dry ground; that we have no form, nor comeliness, nor beauty, that others should desire us; that we have been a nation despised and rejected of men, a nation of sorrows and acquainted with grief. Not only have we not been wounded and bruised for the transgressions of others; but, due to a favorable fortune, we have not always been punished for our own iniquities. As for the saying that "the chastisement of our peace was upon him," it may be true of China with reference to the United States, or of the European peoples with reference to Great Britain; but scarcely can it be thought that we have been chastised for the peace of other nations. For the American people, then, to lay claim to a literal following of the ideal of the Suffering Servant of the Lord would put them in the ludicrous position of that gorbellied knave, Jack Falstaff, who, well filled out with good eating and with good drinking, cries, "A plague of sighing and of grief! It blows a man up like a bladder."

But, while these difficulties must be insuperable for the literalist, they are not altogether so for the pragmatist. It is true that the Suffering Servant of the Lord represents pure goodness without power, and we represent much power with some small measure of goodness. But with that small measure of goodness we may at least give attention to the symbol of the Suffering Servant. For one thing, it is a symbol of responsibility to other nations. For another thing, it suggests that the ultimately prevailing force in the world is spiritual force. And, finally, it lays down suffering and sacrifice, humility and repentance, as the conditions for effective service to the rest of mankind. It is granted that, if we suffer, then our suffering is less than that of the other peoples of the earth. But we may at least strive that such sacrifices as we do make shall be sacrifices toward the cause of Christ, rather than for the empire of Beelzebub; and that, if we cannot be the pre-eminently Suffering Servant of our God, we will, at any rate, be one of the attendants in His retinue.

Of course, for those who insist on bearing the full load of the cross of Christ, this will not do. They are not content, these zealots, with any half-way measures. They will have the whole cross, or none! As a rule, they have their wish: they have none. The undertaking proposed in these pages is a more modest one. It assumes that we are privileged if we are allowed to share a part, however little, of the burden. Herewith, then, some few pieces of the cross to be picked up by our not-too-suffering American servant of the Lord.

### III

In assuming a responsible rôle toward the other nations of the earth, we shall, perhaps, find more specific guidance in a saying of Saint Paul—"We then that are strong ought to bear the infirmities of the weak, and not to please ourselves." * When the strong act so as to please themselves, they usually exploit the infirmities of the weak. But a Christian and democratic heritage summons us to bear those infirmities, and to seek out what we may do to remedy them.

In any case, isolationism is dead as a national policy for the United States. It is time for the American people to grow up. One of the marks of maturity is the willingness to accept responsibility. The infant is not held responsible even for its own actions. As one approaches the condition of an adult, he learns to accept responsibility for what he has done himself. But one has not achieved full moral maturity until he is willing to assume responsibility for consequences which he did not himself bring to pass. This is the case with every responsible parent, with every responsible citizen; and it must be the case with a responsible nation. However, the acceptance of vicarious responsibility for consequences brought to pass by others is no act of supererogation for the simple reason that we constantly, and unthinkingly, accept "responsibility" for the actions of others when those actions bring us enjoyment and good favor. In brief, we complain only of the evils that come to us from others; we do not complain of the free benefits that come to us from them—these benefits are simply taken for granted.

Moreover, we are called on to accept a responsible rôle among the nations of the earth because we have great power as a nation. It may be cruel and tyrannical

* Rom. 15:1.

for a powerful people to use its power so as to exploit other peoples. But it is cowardly and selfish for a powerful people to refrain from exercising its power when its own traditions would direct it to the just use of power. To this extent, the sort of false humility by which we have affected to be unworthy to participate in international judgments has been just a cloak for laziness and for irresponsibility. Indeed, it has been the sin of the American people in international affairs that, in part, they have been ignorant of how much weight they could throw into the balance for justice, and, in part, they have been unwilling to estimate that weight for fear that they might be called upon to toss it on the scales. In any case, it is certain that power will be exercised among the nations by some people or other; and, if we do not put forth our power for justice, then we have no right to take it ill if the injustice set up by another power should finally embrace us in its consequences.

To play a responsible part in the democratic ordering of the world is, of course, not a simple task. The new ordering of the world is a simple task only for Hitler and for Hirohito and for the fascist tyranny. It is simple for tyranny, because tyranny does not propose to take account of the rights of men, of differences in national cultures, and of the great civil and religious liberties by which the human race has made some small measure of progress. For tyranny, it is easy enough to make a blueprint of the "peace." Geopolitics is the master key to the problem, and the Aryan race and the Japanese race are

the master races in the situation, while all other peoples
fall into the appropriate rank of caste and of function
which shall serve the interests of the dominant powers.
Indeed, those who want clarity and precision in the outline of the ideal world order should give their loyalty at
once to the Axis Nations.

The only real clarity that can exist initially in a democratic plan for the re-ordering of the world is a clarity
with reference to guiding principles. These principles are
many, and not one; they provide for individuality, varia-
tion, and growth, as much as for order and stability; they
have to be worked out patiently and experimentally,
rather than put into effect with absolutistic rigor. Their
application calls for qualities of intelligence, vigilance,
open-mindedness, and perseverance; and there will
never be, for the democracies, the comfortable feeling
that might be had by the fascist states that now the basic
pattern has been established, and all one has to do henceforth is to attend to the efficient administration of the
details. This does not mean, of course, that, in the democratic ordering of the world, there will not be specific
programs for specific areas, and specific mechanisms,
political, economic, and technological, to carry out these
programs; but these programs and these mechanisms
will have to have a higher degree of flexibility and of
sensitivity than would be required in a fascist order.

Furthermore, any participation, by the United States,
in a democratic re-ordering of the world will have to be
accompanied by a radical extension of democracy at

home. It is time that we should be done with the artificial distinction between domestic reform and international reform. The two are organically related: when we neglect the international scene, we prepare for an eventual vitiation of our internal reforms; and, unless we give effective illustration of our ideals at home, we cannot expect to impose them on others abroad. This means that we shall have to extend the humanitarian program of the New Deal so far as it makes for the effective promotion of social and economic justice. It calls for an elevation of our standards of literacy, and the broadening of opportunities for advanced education. Above all, it requires that we should make a radical attack upon that fascist canker in our own social structure which is the discrimination against Negroes, and Jews, and Orientals— who are presumed to have equal rights with other American citizens, but whose present disabilities, social, political, and economic, do now stink to high heaven in the very nostrils of God.

As are the British people, so are the American people called upon to liquidate the Tory mind in their spiritual outlook. The Tory mind is one which cares more for the meaning of inherited privileges than for the promise of present opportunities; which regards more the smooth functioning of caste and of class than the vital exchange of communication between free citizens in a growing society; which measures the worth of the individual by his accumulation of wealth, or by his external status of rank and of function, rather than by his productiveness as a good worker and his potentialities as a child of God. The Tory mind thrives as much in a bureaucracy as it does in a plutocracy; it can be found in the ranks of labor leaders as well as in the membership of the American Manufacturers' Association; it corrupts the councils of the church as much as it enters into the smug respectability of a service club. But wherever the Tory mind exists, it mistakes discrimination for equity, prefers vested interests to human rights, confuses material splendor with moral grandeur, dreads progress as disorder, and interprets stagnation as stability.

Nevertheless, no failure at once to fulfill our own domestic destiny, and no hysterical cries of "Imperialism!" should be allowed to divert us from playing our rôle in international reconstruction. For that matter, if there be talk of "imperialism," it must be affirmed unequivocally that there are kinds and degrees of imperialism. Even the leaders of India seem to be dimly aware of this. There are imperialisms that brutally exploit; imperialisms that half exploit and half educate; and imperialisms that literally prepare the way for freedom. To the hyper-sensitive non-interventionist who covers his laziness and irresponsibility with a cloak of Christian charity and humility, these distinctions are as meaningless as, to the anarchist, the differences between a democracy and an autocracy are without significance. All imperialisms are bad, as all governments are intolerable!

However, the United States may be said to have been

justified in its imperialism in the Philippines. It is not justified by any absolute standard: no nation, no individual, is so justified. But it is justified by the relative standards of history. In saying this, I am not ignorant of some of the horrors that were perpetrated during the American occupation of the islands—by natives, as well as by the invaders. Myself, as a young child in China, did often sit, in rapt attention, at the feet of a retired but still tough captain of marines who, in forthright language, would relate how, underneath the starry flag, we civilized 'em with a krag. Yet the facts remain, that the Philippines were granted freedom; that we are fighting now to ensure that freedom; that the people of the Philippines have remained loyal, in this crisis, to their American masters in imperialism; and that we have found, with them, a new fellowship in a common struggle for liberty and for the rights of man. If imperialism can eventuate in this sort of understanding and cooperation between two nations, then it does better than any sanctimonious policy of hands-off and of non-intervention.

It is fruitful, indeed, to compare the spiritual temper of the age of "manifest destiny" in American history with that of the age of pacifism and isolationism. It was the latter period which developed the most caustic criticism of American imperialism, and which held up, as its favorite butt of ridicule, the story of McKinley's prayerfully reaching a decision to take over the burden of administering the Philippines. But what did this later age have to its credit?—the repudiation of the League of Nations, the rejection of the World Court, the Neutrality Act, and that masterpiece of sentimental ineptitude in international relations, the Kellogg-Briand Pact to outlaw war! Measuring the sentimentalism and the hypocrisy of the one era against that of the other, one must prefer the era of "manifest destiny." At any rate, we were, then, alive as a nation; and, if, at times, we betrayed the ideals of democracy, we did so in attempting to extend them, rather than by trying to smother them in our own bosom.

Moreover, the statement that it was primarily financial interests that prompted us to give the Philippines their independence is the sort of glib misrepresentation that only an economist can get away with in our civilization. If all the colonies of every imperialism had been granted independence the minute they became unprofitable ventures from a financial point of view, then half the colonies of the world would have had their independence long ago. Colonies are seized and retained out of motives of national prestige, first of all, and are often held onto in spite of the economic losses they bring. Actually, there were three factors which bore on our emancipation of the Philippines. One of these was our heritage of democratic ideals, which made the idea of imperialism repellent to us. Another was the powerful mood of isolationism in the period after the First World War, whereby we desired to be cut off from all responsibilities to any people beyond our own national boundaries. A third factor was the economic; but, since this factor was present from the very beginning, it obviously cannot have been the decisive one. If we take into account the circumstances in which independence was actually granted to the Philippines, then we are forced to this conclusion: that the long-run, or "first" cause was our heritage of democratic idealism; that the immediate, or "occasional" cause was the mood of isolationism and of irresponsibility in international affairs; and that the alleged economic causes simply provided the sort of sanction which lends respectability to all acts in the culture of Mammonism. In any case, whether for good reasons, or for bad, if we had sense enough to give the Filipinos their independence, then, to just that extent, American imperialism showed itself more sane than other forms of imperialism.

Of course, in the democratic re-ordering of the world after the Second World War, we are not called upon to exercise imperial sway over other peoples. But we are called upon to use force for democratic ends; and we are invited to sit, not with mock humility in the lowest seats of the council, but in such prominent place as may enable us successfully to exert our power for ends that are ideal. To be sure, it is not so uncommon for the individual to use superior force to promote the welfare of others, rather than to exploit their weaknesses; but it is uncommon for a nation to do so. If, then, we who are strong can use our strength, not to please ourselves, but to bear the infirmities of the weak, and to point them toward a path that shall lead them to a strength of body and of spirit that may be equal to our own, and to a fellowship which we may share together in the good things of life, then—if we can do this—we may be justified, as a nation, in some claim upon the title of a servant of the Lord.

## IV

A second task for the United States is to contribute to the moralizing of force—the moralizing of international force. As a political entity, a nation is scarcely the agent of a force that is purely spiritual. If the Jewish people have been a great spiritual force in the world, then it is partly because they do not exist as a political entity. But a nation with a heritage of Christian and of democratic ideals can do something to see that physical force is made the instrument of higher values.

We live, after all, in a world of physical objects which can be acted upon only by physical forces. The ascetic is one who sees the evil in the physical, and withdraws to the realm of the purely spiritual, without attempting to establish any organic interaction between these two aspects of life. For the individual, asceticism may be a partly feasible program, although he can never altogether escape the toils of the flesh; but, for a nation, such a program is quite unthinkable. The middle ages, moreover, show us what happens when asceticism is practiced as a spiritual strategy on a large scale. The result is a social dualism, in which a few may be elected to holiness, but in which the conduct of the practical affairs of the world is turned over to brute power unqualified by any idealism. Indeed, the effect of withdrawing the spiritual from the physical is both the emasculation of the spiritual and the degradation of the physical. A pragmatic strategy, however, will seek to blend these two features in fruitful interaction.

To the naturalist, both Biblical and modern, there can be no evil in physical force in itself. As John Dewey points out, in one of the most significant essays in his *Characters and Events,* the use of force, like the use of any other instrument, is to be judged by its consequences. The consequences of any action include the intended consequence and the collateral consequences. It is in a consideration of the net consequences that we make our judgment. In a world where all judgments are relative, this never allows for pure blame, or for pure praise. At the very best, we are able to say that, at this time, and under these circumstances, this particular course of action, so far as we can see, yields the most desirable net consequences. This does not imply that the end justifies the means; but it does imply that the means are justified by their plural ends, by their several consequences. The use of physical force, then, is warranted, in this world of relative choices, when, at a given time, and under stated circumstances, we find that the use of such force, in a specified manner, will yield a greater net outcome of good than the failure to use it. Naturally, the use of this force calls for correct timing, for discrimination, and for a sense of proportion, as much so as does the use of the surgeon's scalpel.

Accordingly, all talk about mere disarmament after this war must be rejected as too negative in emphasis. Total disarmament is essentially the strategy of spiritual asceticism in international relations, promulgated, now, by a generation that is neither spiritually nor ascetically minded, but which, with the instinct of an unerring sentimentalism, reaches after that strategy which, apparently, will yield it the maximum of comfort with the minimum expenditure of effort and of pain. In the decade of the twenties, however, the American people had a good example of what happens when a domestic police force is inadequately armed. The lawless elements still kept up-to-date their own armaments, and we were ridden with gangsterism from one coast to the other. It was not until the men of the Federal Bureau of Investigation were equipped with more modern and more scientific devices for fighting and for crime detection that we began to have some relief from this menace. If the outlaw is still with us in our domestic economy, then we are still less justified in believing that, by the conclusion of this war, he will automatically disappear from the infinitely less well ordered realm of international relations. For many years to come, we must expect the emergence of gangster groups in the society of nations. And we shall cope with them, not by eliminating our armaments, but by making our armaments more scientifically efficient, and by placing them in the hands of men of intelligence, integrity, and ability.

If this policy is followed, then it is quite possible that annual conscription of our men for military training will become as much a part of our peace-time program as it has been for European peoples. Whether or not such action is necessary is a matter for experimental testing. But, in any case, we need pay no attention to the protest that conscription promotes the military mind in a citizenry. On the contrary, the conscription of a citizen army is precisely the way a democracy can give itself full military protection, without surrendering to the military mind. The real menace lies in a large, standing, professional army, the members of which may forget the ideals of the state which they serve. But the members of a citizen army always think of themselves first as citizens, who, for the time being, may be doing their duty in military service, but who expect to return, shortly, to their ordinary occupations as doctors, laborers, teachers, executives, clerks, and the like. This sort of soldier is less likely to forget the pacific and humanitarian ideals which are the meaning of democracy than the soldier who, all his adult life, has known nothing but military discipline. Switzerland is one good instance in favor of this thesis, and democratic France would have been an instance if her officer caste had not been so largely dominated by the aristocratic traditions of the *ancien régime*. Furthermore, with regard to that minimum number of professional soldiers which is indispensable for the maintenance of any effective fighting force, the problem is no more acute than that of controlling the police force in a democracy.

Of course, there are those who argue that an army has no resemblance to a police force. A police force, they say, does not engage in wholesale slaughter; it does not practise the indiscriminate killing of civilian populations; it does not destroy cities, churches, museums, hospitals, art galleries, and all the other tokens and repositories of human civilization. It is not the instrument by which a powerful and predatory group imposes its will on others, and exploits the weaknesses of less favorably endowed peoples. A police force is the instrument of order, peace, and decency; a mechanism whereby law-abiding citizens are protected in the pursuit of their rightful functions while lawless elements are held in abeyance.

But such an argument could be advanced only by the absolutist, with his characteristic contempt for the facts of history. On the contrary, there are few police forces which have not been used to perpetrate just that destruction of civilized values which is alleged to be the function only of an army. The present German *Gestapo* is an excellent case in point. Indeed, it is probable that the *Gestapo* has done more to destroy human liberties and human life than the German army. And it is interesting to note that the citizens of Nazi-occupied countries seem to prefer the rule of the army to the rule of the *Gestapo*. Nations other than Germany, however, have had police systems that were instruments of tyranny. The Spanish

Inquisition, the tzarist secret police, and the *Ogpu* are hardly to be listed as staunch defenders of human liberties. Nor need Americans search their memories long and hard to recall instances when our metropolitan police were used in deliberate acts of brutality, and when our national guard was customarily employed to shoot down strikers and to terrorize their families, although its force was never directed against the employer and the capitalist. Certainly, it would make the subject of an interesting inquiry, to determine whether, in the total record, there has been more destruction of human life and of civil liberties in the spectacular struggles of large armies, or in the quieter and more deadly work of an efficient and tyrannical police.

Fortunately, however, in domestic affairs, we have never been such anarchists as to believe that the solution to the problem of a corrupt and tyrannical police was to abolish the police system altogether. Yet it is just such a strategy of spiritual asceticism which is recommended by some persons for the international scene. It makes about as much sense as though, in an industrial city, discovering that the air was polluted by the smoke of the factories, one should recommend that the citizens quit breathing air altogether. It is true that, to the extent that the American people have acted on a tradition of distrust of the governmental power as a tool of tyranny, they have not always armed their police adequately and supported them properly in the courts of justice. And we have suffered for it, in domestic lawlessness and gangsterism. But we are gradually learning that a police force, if it is to function at all, must be efficiently trained and armed. And we have long believed that the solution to the problem of a tyrannical police is, not to abolish the police, but to moralize the police power.

After this war, we are called upon to bear our part in a similar task in the international scene. We are called upon to aid in moralizing armies and navies, so that they cease to be instruments of national tyranny, and are converted into mechanisms for preserving international law and order and peace. The international problem differs from the domestic problem chiefly in a quantitative sense. And, if it has taken us many centuries to make a little headway in moralizing our domestic police system, then we must expect to exercise similar patience and perseverance in moralizing an international police. Undoubtedly, such a police, at the beginning, will be a tool in the hands of the powers that be. This is true of the origin of any police system. But it will make a great difference to the world whether the powers that originate this authority are initially disposed to confirm old privileges with new wrongs, and to deepen distinctions of race, and caste, and creed, or are disposed to work toward a world of human brotherhood that shall be in accord with a Christian and a democratic heritage of ideals. The American people, with their great resources of material and of moral power, cannot fail to play a part in this undertaking.

In conclusion, here, let me say that I am not unaware

that there is a certain high irony in identifying the Suffering Servant with an armed international policeman. But I am inclined to think that a conscientious policeman, who knows his duty and is willing to die for it, finds more favor in the sight of the Lord than the indolent and irresponsible citizen who sits smugly at home and neither serves nor suffers. And I should rather be the citizen of a nation which, at least taking some clue from its Christian heritage, should act upon that clue to the best of its ability, than be the citizen of a nation which, finding that it cannot live up to the full requirements of the law of Christ, should reject both the spirit and the letter of that law, in a hypocritical posture of mock humility and of self-deprecation.

v

There is, however, an opportunity for the American people to experience some real suffering—suffering, that is, according to the criterion of supreme value in the culture of Mammonism. We can learn to cut down on our national prosperity, to surrender some measure of our well-beloved high standard of living. We must do this, if we are to play our part in rehabilitating the other peoples of the earth, and in laying a sure foundation for the peace of the future.

Even as I write, the press carries a front-page report of a recent address by the national president of the United States Chamber of Commerce. The headline reads, "Great Prosperity Period Predicted After Victory!" The spokesman is described as a youthful and dynamic individual—the youngest ever to hold his office. He is reported as saying that one reason why the Germans have been so successful in the war is that they know what they are fighting for. Apparently they are fighting for *lebensraum*. The Russians, too, display great valor, because they are fighting for a "new day." The inference to be drawn from the rest of the discourse seems to be that Americans, also, must know what they are fighting for, and that what they are fighting for is a return of the prosperity of the good measure, pressed down, and shaken together, and running over. And there are listed six sound reasons in economics as to why we may expect this outcome for our efforts in the war.

The sentiments here expressed are of a sort that must appeal to every decent and right-thinking American citizen. We should be reluctant, of course, to say that our young men are being called upon to die on foreign battlefields, in order to guarantee to the rest of us the enjoyment, in perpetuity, of an extra lump of sugar in our coffee and of a spare tire to our automobiles. But, then, virtue must have its reward; and the only reward that is tangible, and appreciable by all men, is the reward of material abundance. Is it not written that, if ye seek first the Kingdom of God, then all these other things shall be added unto you? Surely, we are justified in expecting, after the Second World War, a prosperity boom that shall be similar to what we enjoyed after the First

World War. Only, this time we must take care that our prosperity rests on a more enduring foundation than it did before.

One cannot criticize the national president of the Chamber of Commerce for being concerned with the problem of economic adjustment in this country after the war. That is his business. But so far as his address is a statement of the ideal outcome of the war—and it is for too many of us—it is as thoroughly immoral a statement as could be formulated. To this extent, it reflects the hold, upon the American mind, of the great fetich of prosperity. Doubt the belief in God, the hope of salvation, the love of humanity—but doubt never that Providence, in its dispensations, has decreed prosperity for the American people *in saecula saeculorum*! Just as Hitler has made national power his absolute, and has believed that, from it, all blessings should flow; just as the pacifist makes peace his absolute, and feels confident that it is the foundation of all other good things; so Americans have tended to make an absolute out of prosperity, and to think that, when it is assured, then justice, mercy, and faithfulness must follow after, as inevitably as the day the night.

Certainly, there is a problem of economic re-adjustment after the war; but it is not just an American problem. Often enough we have been told that there can be no effective and enduring peace until all peoples of the earth are guaranteed equal access to markets and to raw materials, and are free to engage in the exchange of goods and services with one another unhampered by artificial trade barriers. There is industry to be rebuilt in other countries; there are farm lands to be reclaimed from the devastation of war; there are communications to be set in order, cities to be raised again, millions of hungry mouths to be fed, and millions of diseased bodies to be nourished back to health. Yet, during all this work of reconstruction, we are to be enjoying prosperity!

Of course, the economists, with their inevitable optimism, will paint a rosy picture of the whole proceeding. This will be the time for them to fetch out, from their libraries, the arguments, long covered by the dust of disuse, in favor of free trade; and to launch forth into another glowing description of the utopia that shall come to mankind when every nation produces according to its resources and abilities, sells in an open market, and purchases from other countries only those commodities which it cannot efficiently grow or manufacture for itself. As a pure exercise in metaphysical idealism, this sort of talk is, doubtless, to be commended. And, if it all rests on wishful thinking, then it is the sort of wishful thinking that is regarded as respectable in the *mores* of Mammonism.

But the American people should be quite clear what such a program means to their own economy. It means sacrifice. And I do not mean "sacrifice" in the economist's sense of capital invested to yield an early and assured material return, but I mean sacrifice, in the ethical sense, of goods and services surrendered without much expectation of a reward that is other than spiritual. After all, we are Dives to the Lazarus that is the rest of the world; and, by the conclusion of this war, the dainties that are heaped on our own tables will be more than ever as nectar and ambrosia compared to the crumbs for which the beggar peoples scramble in the barren outer courts. Under these circumstances, the immediate effect of making free and open the channels of trade may be to bring more comfort and decency to the lazzarones, but not to make Dives richer. And, if Dives wants to console himself with the thought that, some time in the future, living in a whole society of able-bodied citizens, he may enjoy still more comfort and prosperity than he does now, this hope should not blind him to the reality that, for the present, and for some time to come, his chief experience must be one of sacrifice, and not of surfeit. Moreover, should Dives' private chaplain, the economist, assure him that, by graduating the scale of his philanthropies over several years, he can, at the same time, attend to his own prosperity and to the well-being of his fellowmen, the chances are that, after a few generous efforts, he will simply relapse into his customary self-contentment, while the beggars without grow more savage in a conflict that must eventually consume them, and him, too.

The lesson the American people have to learn here may be a bitter one, and, unquestionably, it will provide the crucial test in our post-war policy. For, if we proceed to look at once for a return of national prosperity, then our attention will be diverted from the needs of the other peoples of the earth. Those needs, moreover, will not be of a sort the satisfaction of which can be graduated over a period of years. They will be immediate needs and crying needs—for food, for clothing, for shelter, for medical care, for skilled helpers and for technical supervisors; and the nation that plays nurse to those needs will not sacrifice and suffer to the necessary degree if it thinks chiefly of its own comfort and well-being. Let the economists and utopians, if they like, dazzle us with the vision of material rewards in the heaven of a future time; but let the religionists and the realists concentrate upon the present imperative for giving, for giving without stint, and for giving without hope of return. There is a price for victory in peace, as for victory in war; and we must pay it. And the blessings of peace are, not first of all prosperity, but justice, mercy, and faithfulness, and the surer knowledge that our own offspring shall not be caught in another catastrophe that shall be worse than what we have known.

There is, of course, in the traditions of the American people, a habit which may be ample enough and strong enough to rise to this emergency. It is the habit of philanthropy. Our civilization has produced, in abundance, Aristotle's Magnificent Man, as, also, his Man of Vulgar Profusion—men who could give freely of their money to others, either in good taste, or in bad; but it has not produced many of the Niggard, or of the Skinflint type. The character of the miser, so familiar in other literatures, is almost a stranger to our own. We have not been a nation of nickel-nursers; and, if there have been among us some who were a bit close with their pennies, then, as with the Jew and the Scotchman, it was only in order to be the more generous in their philanthropies. Moreover, with us, the habit of philanthropy has not been just an automatic reflex of prosperity: it could never be that, for there is nothing in the mere fact of wealth to make a man generous. It has been, rather, a Christian and a democratic discipline imposed upon the culture of Mammonism.

Yet it is true that prosperity has usually been there to make this custom easier. Most of us do not yet know what it is to give in the spirit of the widow's mite, for we have usually cast into the Lord's treasury out of our abundance. In any case, whether we give as widows, or as men of wealth, let us fix our attention first of all upon justice, and peace, and brotherhood; and if we must dream of prosperity, let us think of it as an alleviation of the needs of those who are in want, or as a blessing which our children's children may enjoy without worshiping it as we have.

VI

It has been pointed out that the miracle in the book of *Jonah* lies, not in the story of the great fish, but in the repentance of the people of Nineveh. One can appreciate the resentment of the prophet, that the Lord should allow such a thing to come to pass. Let Jehovah call down fire from heaven, or summon strange monsters from the deep; let Him bring the dead back to life, or halt the sun and the moon in their courses: but, when He permits a whole nation to be overcome with humility for its sins, and to repent in sackcloth and in ashes, He is exceeding the limits of probability which make prophecy a reasonably calculable practice.

Within limits, a democracy is a state where the miracle of the book of *Jonah* can be re-enacted. For the democratic theory of the state is an ethical theory which denies that politics is only a competition for power, and which affirms that the state exists to serve certain ideal values such as liberty, fraternity, and justice. The state, moreover, is held to be but one of several vital forms of human association and must find its appropriate place in company with the family, the church, the school, and the pursuits of business. Under these circumstances, it is possible to bring the state under the moral judgments of high religion. At the present moment, for instance, it is noteworthy that so many of the Christian clergy in the Anglo-American democracies are more concerned to bring the people to a sense of sin, than to build up their pride in armaments and their confidence of ultimate military victory. And while it may be a question whether all the people of Britain and of America—like the people of Nineveh—shall ever come to repent profoundly of their misdeeds, it is, nevertheless, significant that, in these states, there is some provision for the cultivation of humility.

The national rituals of humility vary from one democracy to another. Americans, for instance, are always fascinated by this ritual as it is periodically performed by the British Prime Minister. It would seem that, every now and then, the Prime Minister is called upon to appear before Parliament, and to make a confession of sin; and if he confesses to enough mistakes, and to big enough mistakes, and bears himself manfully in his errors, he is given an overwhelming vote of confidence, and guaranteed in the further tenure of his office. Such behavior on the part of an American statesman would be held by us to be politically scandalous. But the British Government is one that has learned to admit that it can make mistakes, and the British people have learned to place more confidence in the integrity of a leader who is honest enough to confess his errors, than in the pretenses of a dictator who should lay claim to absolute infallibility.

In the United States, as a younger nation, the rituals of humility are not yet so clearly defined. Our behavior, till recent times, has exhibited the ambivalence of the conduct of an adolescent. On the one hand, there has been a sort of bumptiousness and boastfulness as of a young people that glories in the exercise of its strength, but has not yet measured that strength with the strength of other peoples often enough to achieve a mature understanding of its own powers. On the other hand, we have displayed an extraordinary—and, at times, unseemly—humility in the presence of those who told us they were our superiors in cultural attainments. The visiting foreign lecturer—were he Hindu mystic, or English man-of-letters, or German philosopher—soon discovered, if he was alert at his business, that the amount of the fee he could command rose in exact proportion to the number of insults he could heap upon our civilization.

But genuine humility for us as a people is not to be found by paying deference to the accomplished snobbery of the self-appointed emissaries of cultural enlightenment. There are good signs, indeed, that we are already sick of performing these fruitless obeisances. Genuine humility is always humility evoked by the presence of the ideal. It means the realization of how little we have done compared to what we might have done, and of how poorly we have lived up to the noblest imperatives in our own spiritual heritage. Standing in judgment before our heritage of democratic ideals, let us repent of our domestic betrayals of liberty, of justice, and of fraternity, and of that selfish isolationism whereby we would have kept to ourselves those good things which originally came to us from others. Standing in judgment before our heritage of Christian ideals, let us repent of all these matters again, and repent also of the materialism, the hedonism, the sentimentalism, and the complacency, with which we have corrupted the image of God in ourselves into the likeness of the man that is only carnal.

At this moment, more than at any other, we are in need of such humility. For, at this moment, we are as a city that is set on an hill, and so cannot be hid. Yet it is the hill which lends eminence and visibility—the hill of high aspiration after liberty, and justice, and truth. And the city that is set on the hill can also be cast down into the plain, should that city be proved unfit to cling to such soaring heights. The inhabitants of this city, verily, are Abraham's seed and God's elect. But they are the elect only so long as they walk on the cool peaks, and do not tumble into the warm and pleasant valley. Should they forsake their dwelling on the mountain-top, then out of the very stones shall God raise up new seed to Abraham.

Whether or not, then, the American people shall prove worthy of their present eminence, is a question of how true they can be to their own heritage of Christian and of democratic ideals. It is doubtless so, that, as a nation, we can never measure up to the full stature of the Suffering Servant of the Lord. Like other peoples, we have our human weaknesses, and commit our share of human errors. But, if to err is human, the human approaches the divine when it errs in the right direction. And, if err we must, then let us err in the direction of the ideal of that nation of which it may be said:

> A bruised reed will he not break,
>   And a dimly burning wick will he not quench.
> He will bring forth justice in truth.
>   He will not fail nor be discouraged,
> Till he have set justice in the earth.

# Index

177

Hymns, 97
Hypocrisy, 17, 156

Idealism, 17, 22, 24, 31, 52, 56, 57,
  59, 63, 64, 78, 127–128, 174
Imperialism, 81, 154–158
India, 58–59, 146, 147, 154
Individual, 26, 32, 62, 80
Inquisition, Spanish, 163
International Relations, chaps. II, V
Isaiah, 141, 148, 175
Isolationism, chap. II; 4, 80, 144,
  150, 155, 156–157, 174
Italy, 7

Jackson, Andrew, 115
James, William, 128, 137
Japan, 13, 14, 21, 57, 58, 76, 111,
  134
Jefferson, Thomas, 115
Jesus Christ, 2, 32, 46, 51, 52, 53, 75,
  76, 97, 99, 132, 147, 149, 165
Jews, 4, 22, 114, 153, 158, 171
*Job*, 82
*John,* gospel of, 2
Johnson, Senator, 62
*Jonah*, 75, 171–172
Justice, 24, 52, 55, 60, 78, 97, 114,
  136, 139, 170, 172, 175

Kagawa, 57–58
Kant, Immanuel, 99, 100
Kellogg-Briand Pact, 156

Labor, 19, 25, 62, 154, 163
*Laissez-faire,* ix, 21, 25, 37, 126, 135
Lawrence, D. H., 45
Lazarus, cf. Dives and Lazarus
League of Nations, 114, 156
*Lebensraum,* 7, 112, 166
Leibnitz, 79

Lewis, John L., 25
Liberty, 16, 20, 21, 25, 63, 78, 107,
  114, 115, 136, 139, 151, 163, 172
Lincoln, 33, 88, 129
Lindbergh, Charles, 19–20
Locke, John, 137
Logic, 82–83, 85–86, 89–93
Love, 15, 32, 33, 44, 45, 51, 52, 55,
  56, 97–98, 135, 170
Loyola, Ignatius, 48
Lucretius, 65, 101
*Luke,* gospel of, 2, 103–104
Luther, Martin, 133

Machiavelli, 63
Mandeville, 79
Mammonism, chap. I; ix–x, 51, 109,
  110, 113, 129, 132, 157, 165, 168,
  171
Manifest Destiny, 155–156
Marcus Aurelius, 33
Marx, Karl, x
Materialism, cf. Mammonism
Mathematics, 85, 87
*Matthew,* gospel of, 35–36
McKinley, President, 155
Means and Ends, 130, 159
Mencius, 82
Metaphysics, cf. Economics
Methodists, 125
Mexico, 111
Middle Ages, 7, 8, 46, 158
Middle classes, cf. Bourgeois
Mill, J. S., 9–10, 14
Mind, 5, 15, 16, 31, 50, 74, 88, 100
Miracles, 11, 172
Missions, 48, 49–50
Mohammedanism, 46, 145
Monasticism, 48–49, 64
Morale, 20
Morals, 59, 61–62, 78–80